A WAY OUT OF NO WAY

MIRACULOUS STUFF YOU CAN'T MAKE UP

Ronnie L. Parson

BW *Broad Wing Press* ©

Lanham, MD

A Way out of No Way: Miraculous Stuff You Can't Make Up

ISBN: 978-1967034-20-8

Unless otherwise noted, Scripture is taken from the New American Standard Bible, Copyright © 1960, 1962, 1963, 1968, 1971, 1972, 1973, 1975, 1979 by the Lockman Foundation.

Table of Content

DEDICATION

This book is dedicated to the memory of Bishop Ralph Lee White. I will forever be grateful to him for all he has meant to me, my family, and the ministry of the Living Church of Our Lord Jesus Christ. Bishop White allowed this young man to grow and mature in ministry. Because he supported my efforts to be all that God called me to be, I stand today in a place of grace with great responsibility. Bishop Ralph Lee White was known for his physical strength, but the power of his character was even more robust. I dedicate this book to the one who gave me strong shoulders to stand on in the early days of ministry. During a time when sinking sand was everywhere, I stepped.

FORWORD

I grew up in church, so trusting the Lord for everything has been with me for as long as I can remember. My mother instilled church in me as a little boy, and her passing from leukemia devastated me, but I knew she loved the Lord. It was through the church that I came to know Dr. Parson, and it has been great seeing how God uses him to inspire others. He is not selfish with his gifts and talents, but uses them to encourage people to know this God he preaches about and lives for. Dr. Parson isn't just about preaching and teaching the word; he is about winning souls for the kingdom. He continues to look up because that is where his help comes from: His support comes from the Lord.

It is not easy serving as a pastor or in any leadership position because people are people, and will challenge your integrity. I witnessed something of that nature years ago when Dr. Parson could have lost his sanity, but did not. God took control while he kept looking up. I encourage you that know the Lord and those who have not come to know him yet to read this inspiring and motivating book. It is a witness to the reality that looking up works. Because "stuff is going to happen" that we cannot make up. Stuff that sometimes sends us into a panic, and we lose all sense of reality. But this book inspires us to look up to God when stuff happens. He is right there! We do not have to lean on our understanding.

Direction for our path is a matter of acknowledging God in all our ways.

This book motivates us by showing how God delivers time and time again. Things that could have happened didn't (a God moment). Reading testimony after testimony of God's sovereignty, protection, and provision motivates one to trust God for more incredible things. If you are a believer, and if you are not, start trusting Him right now. Then, when the stuff you can't make up happen, whether you want to admit it or not, you find yourself looking for help from a God who has never let you down. He is a very present help in a time of trouble. We all go through stuff, and He will not abandon any of us in those moments of desperation. Acts 10:34-35 affirms that: *Of a truth, I perceive that God is no respecter of persons: But in every nation, he that feareth him, and worketh righteousness, is accepted with him.* Go ahead and read this book; you will agree with me. What a Mighty God we serve!

Deacon Ralph Wilson, Sr.

PREFACE

As I get older and a younger, more savvy internet social media generation matures, I frequently find that I am in discussions with those presenting philosophical arguments attacking the Christian faith. I've heard several arguments: "Christians are serving and worshipping the wrong God," "Jesus was not God," The real Hebrews are not Jews, "Jesus was a fabrication from African Historical folklore," and the classic one" religion was thought up as a way to scare ordinary people into submission to dominant powers."

Indeed, with global access to the internet, the list seems to have no end. It is saturated with demonizing information that is mainly fueling this attempt to burn down the Christian faith. Anybody, whether they are trained in research or not, can put together an anti-Christian argument from information on the web.

Yet, with all the available information, there is one missing component that answers why Christianity still exists and will always exist. The Christian faith is surrounded by a firewall of the "resurrection of Jesus Christ." The firewall of the resurrection has kept Christianity standing strong for over 2000 years. The Apostle Paul sums it up best.

If in this life only we have hope in Christ, we are of all men the most pitiable. But now Christ is risen from the dead and has become the first fruits of those who have fallen asleep. (1 Cor 15:19-20).

Jesus, the head of the church, is alive! Even in medical science, doctors won't pull the plug on a patient on life support unless they are brain-dead. No matter what crashes into Christianity and attempts to leave it on life support, the devil will never be able to pull the plug. Jesus is the life support of the church—-His body. Jesus is not dead; therefore, the church is not brain-dead. The church will remain on life support until the Lord Jesus Christ returns.

And when I saw Him, I fell at His feet as dead. But He laid His right hand on me, saying to me, "Do not be afraid; I am the First and the Last. I am He who lives, and was dead, and behold, I am alive forevermore. Amen. And I have the keys of Hades and of Death. (Rev 1:17-18)

Jesus, the inaugurator and creator of the new covenant, was dead, but now He is alive forever and continues to work in the lives of those who are in union with Him. Orthodox Christians agree that, like philosophies throughout history that have dissolved into obscurity, without this firewall of the resurrection, the Christian faith would have crashed and burned long ago. Yet this faith withstands severe attacks, not because of a sure "philosophy" to argue and debate, but it is built on an infallible word of prophecy that has withstood the onslaughts of the test of time. Apostle Peter, who was an active part of the earthly ministry of Jesus, wrote:

> *For we did not follow cunningly devised fables when we made known to you the power and coming of our Lord Jesus Christ, but were eyewitnesses of His majesty. For He received from God the Father honor and glory when such a voice came to Him from the Excellent Glory: "This is My beloved Son, in whom I am well pleased. And we heard this voice which came from heaven when we were with Him on the holy mountain. And so we have the prophetic word confirmed, which you do well to heed as a light that shines in a dark place, until the day dawns and the morning star rises in your hearts; knowing this first, that no prophecy of Scripture is of any private interpretation, for prophecy never came by the will of man, but holy men of God spoke as they were moved by the Holy Spirit.* (2 Ptr 1:16-21)

Those coming up with new ways to attack Christianity are missing the essential point that it is far more than a mere religion based on philosophical arguments. It is founded on a relationship with Jesus Christ, the son of the living God (Matt. 16:16). Jesus was born of a real virgin, by the will of God. He lived, died, and rose from the grave, and His Spirit lives on in the hearts and souls of Spirit-filled believers who are the principal witnesses to his resurrection. For He is actively working in their lives through the person of the Holy Spirit.

This book divulges some of my experiences in seeing God do the amazing. He has been actively at work in my life, and as much as I allow Him, He continues to order my steps.

A Christian's witness is not subject to disputes. Nor can it be disproven by the latest discoveries that allegedly confirm that Christians are serving the wrong God. However, younger generations sometimes think they have uncovered answers that previous generations missed and need to know.

Most of us have probably felt this way toward our parents at some point lives. But conjured, or surfed up, sophisticated presentations are rooted in age-old arguments that have persisted for generations.

Yet, I am only one among countless believers throughout Christian history who can share stories of triumph. These believers dedicate their lives to serving the risen Christ, who continues to act in extraordinary ways— ways that are far too remarkable to be dismissed as coincidence or mere chance.

Yes, without the safeguard of the firewall of the resurrection, even Scripture acknowledges that Christians would be left with a worldview similar to that of the hopeless Epicurean philosophers. The Apostle Paul makes it clear that if the resurrection did not occur,

Christians might as well approach life like the Epicurean philosophers, when he admonishes,

> *If, in the manner of men, I have fought with beasts at Ephesus, what advantage is it to me? If the dead do not rise, "Let us eat and drink, for tomorrow we die!" Do not be deceived: "Evil company corrupts good habits.* (1 Cor 15:32-33)

He spoke in response to members of the first-century Corinthian church. Some had begun to say there was no such thing as the resurrection from the dead. But the Christian faith has never been a mere religion based on a well-thought-out philosophy and open to well-crafted arguments of well-learned individuals. One of the most intelligent and inspired men mentioned in the Bible concludes that God's foolishness is wiser than man's wisdom.

> *… but we preach Christ crucified, to the Jews a stumbling block and to the Greeks foolishness, but to those who are called, both Jews and Greeks, Christ the power of God and the wisdom of God. Because the foolishness of God is wiser than men, and the weakness of God is stronger than men.* (1 Cor 1:23-25)

I encourage all believers to memorialize the ways our Lord Jesus is alive and actively at work in their lives daily.

The son of the Living God continues to operate in His disciples' lives in ways they cannot conjure up.

In this first volume, I began documenting what I have experienced of His divine protection, providence, and provision. In doing so, I desire to help future generations keep looking up, no matter what a satanically driven population conjures up to distort reality and deceive anyone too distracted by a complicated world that appears to be failing at every turn. Eternal life does not await the believers. Believers are living eternal life now because we serve a Living God who is actively and consistently at work in our lives.

> *The thief's purpose is to steal, kill and destroy. My purpose is to give life in all its fullness.* (Jn 10:10)

> *And I am sure that God who began the good work within you will keep right on helping you grow in his grace until his task within you is finally finished on that day when Jesus Christ returns* (Phil 1:6)

INTRODUCTION

Turn to me and be saved, all you ends of the earth; for I am God, and there is no other. (Isa 45:22, NIV)

I am the LORD: that is my name: and my glory will I not give to another, neither my praise to graven images (Isa 42:8)

I love the word of God, but what stands out most is the stuff you can't make up! It is a collection of 66 books written by those who were moved or inspired by the Holy Spirit, yet the storyline is cohesive and flows perfectly, with everything fitting together. Although there are errors in some translations, the canon of scripture itself is inerrant. The obvious and simple explanation for its inerrancy is that holy men spoke as they were moved by the Holy Spirit (2 Pet. 1:21). Also, the Bible has one author, God. The Christian Bible is the infallible word of God! Therefore, the Bible is profitable and irreplaceable for anyone seeking to know God and experience salvation, and is required to inhabit the kingdom of God that is growing even in our world today.

There is no chance that several authors could write one book over centuries, and the storyline fits perfectly together. Although the Bible contains some scientific facts, it is not a science textbook but a salvation story. The Bible doesn't care about defining the age of the world.

And neither is the Bible concerned with why dinosaurs became extinct. The Bible gives what is needed for the world to escape perishing and have everlasting life. If science proves that the world is a trillion years old or discovers that it's six thousand years old, the Bible does not care. If science proves that dinosaurs were destroyed by a meteorite or some other cataclysmic event, the Bible does not care. What the Bible does care about is instructing its readers in righteousness. In giving the history of salvation and examples of those who played intricate roles, the scripture shows God at work in ways that a human mind could not think up. There is no comparing God's thoughts and methods to ours. As Isaiah noted:

> For My thoughts are not your thoughts, Nor are your ways My ways," says the LORD. "For as the heavens are higher than the earth, So are My ways higher than your ways, And My thoughts than your thoughts. (Isa 55:8-9 NKJV)

God's ways and thoughts are phenomenal and lead to unthinkable outcomes. To say that God is a creative thinker is putting it mildly. There is no searching His understanding

The bible contains scientific facts, but it is not a science book, it's a salvation story.

(Isa 40:28), and His ways are past finding out (Rom 11:33).

Over time, I have learned that God is the master of blessing in innovative ways that cannot be imagined: in ways we never saw coming. His provision and protection in times of need leave no doubt that He is providential in working on our behalf. His impeccable timing makes His glory irrefutable.

The unimaginable happened so much in my life that I found myself repeating the expression, "you can't make this stuff up." It has caught on, and those around me are now saying the same thing: God continues to work in our lives in ways unmatched by anything we could accomplish without Him. The words *accident* and *incident* fall short of explaining what is apparent due to divine providence. Every time I hear someone say. "He made a way out of no way," the word of Jesus enters my mind:

> *Jesus said to him, I am the way, the truth, and the life. No one comes to the Father except through Me.* (Jn 14:6)

Jesus personifies the way to God and every other way that makes human life the way God created it. God's ways, recorded in scripture, are the practices necessary for daily living. Those who are united to Jesus have no limitations because God makes all things possible.

> *The thief's purpose is to steal, kill and destroy. My purpose is to give life in all its fullness* (Jn 10:10 TLB)

Those who commit their life to Jesus will always have the right way. However, they must trust God's timing and His process to complete a thing. Ultimately, we win but must go through the process of arriving.

PUTTING OUR PUZZLE TOGETHER

Our lives are like a puzzle that God is putting together over time. The outside of a puzzle box displays a photograph of the puzzle in the box. All the pieces of the puzzle are in the box, but until it is completely assembled, it's still like an unfolding mystery. The small pieces of life fit into the whole; we do not have to add or make pieces. Like the puzzle, the necessary pieces for the finished work are there. The details of our lives are set, and they fit together perfectly. Only God is omniscient, so He alone knows how to fit these pieces together. Though we win in the end, in the meantime, the purpose for our lives comes together piece by piece over time.

God works in us and through us, and if you want to know your purpose, study your life, because God has been working it out all the time. With Him, there are no incidents that are accidents. It's happening according to his divine providence. For those who love the Lord, the puzzle pieces are already in our lives. There are no missing or extra pieces. We are complete in Jesus. There are no pieces that almost fit.

> **If you want to know your purpose study your life because God has been doing it all of your life.**

4

For as Scripture tells us, *All things work together for good for those who love God* (Rom 8:28). The result will be a picture of a perfect purpose, like a perfectly completed puzzle. So, finally, what was puzzling and unknown about our experiences was always well known to God and will eventually be known to us. In the meantime, we must keep looking up in faith.

We trust Him who knows how the pieces of our lives fit together because the entire trajectory of our lives is well known to Him, like the picture on the outside of a box full of puzzle pieces. Every life is precious to God, and those who allow Him will experience all His thoughts and ways that always lead to good, even when life seems wrong. God shows himself in ways that only he can do.

Making an indisputable statement is God's specialty. He knows how to stamp his identity on what he does. So much so that "to God be the glory" is the proper and only response that makes any sense. I've seen God do things that I could have never come up with on my own. These experiences have led me to say, you can't make this stuff up. Even if I sit down and think about it for a lifetime. There is a biblical reason for this. Scripture clearly teaches that God will not share His glory with anyone else. Isaiah 42:8, declares,

I am the LORD; that is my name; my glory I give to no other, nor my praise to carved idols"

All honor, splendor, and praise belong to God alone, and He will not allow His glory to be attributed to false gods, idols made of stone, wood, or clay, or humans. This underscores the absolute uniqueness and supremacy of God, making it clear that He alone is worthy of ultimate glory and worship.

So, God makes his glory irrefutable by being at work in our lives. And, at least for me, it would take more faith to be an atheist than to *believe in God and believe God*. Some people believe in God, but their response to His written word suggests that they don't believe God.

Through Isaiah, God makes it clear that he protects his reputation, does not tolerate plagiarism, nor allows others to take his praise. I decided to write this book to encourage some and remind others that everything that occurs in the world is well known to the one who created it. Our lives are no exception, as Job says:

Everything about us is in the puzzle box of eternity. God fits the pieces together in time.

> *But He knows the way that I take; When He has tested me, I shall come forth as gold* .(Job 23:10)

This book contains examples of occurrences in my life that affirm how the Lord put pieces of my life puzzle together. Again, everything about us is in the puzzle box of eternity, and only God can fit the pieces perfectly together in time. The right timing makes the right thing beautiful.

With so many seeking to discredit Christ and Christianity, one timeless, ironclad reality is that God continues to work in our lives. I often meet people who present philosophical arguments about religion, claiming to have

evidence that believers are either worshipping the wrong God or following a myth. Yet, real-life experiences and events always stand as undeniable proof—something these arguments can never fully refute or explain away.

I speak of the countless testimonies that bear witness to how the God of the Bible continually remains actively involved in our lives to assure divine protection, provision, and providence. There may come a time when the blood of the Lamb and unwavering testimonies of believers may be the only defense future generations have against challenges to the truth of Christianity. As Peter affirmed, the word of God remains our steadfast assurance of His existence. Yet, it is also clear that the God of scripture is the same God who faithfully works in our lives day after day and year after year.

> *He has made everything beautiful in its time. He has also set eternity in the human heart; yet no one can fathom what God has done from beginning to end.* (Eccl 3:11)

DIVINE PROTECTION, PROVIDENCE & PROVISION

For now we see in a mirror, dimly, but then face to face...
(1 Cor 13:12a)

Before global positioning satellites (GPS), taking a road trip into an unfamiliar city was time-consuming. One could easily get lost with or without a map. It could be puzzling sometimes, especially when streets were blocked and roadways were under construction. Because there is "no new thing under the sun" (Eccl 1:9), we often say, " I've been down this road before. For me, the Deja vu moments seem to increase with age. Such is life. Life is a journey that begins in uncertainty and often leads us through unpredictable and challenging terrains. However, when we allow God to guide us and be our navigational expert, the journey becomes a matter of faith in His promises. All that is uncertain and puzzling is part of His providence —carefully crafted to protect and provide for those who love Him.

God rains on all and causes His sun to shine on all the same. However, those who love Him will experience inexplicable encounters and interventions. They will survive car accidents that take the lives of others. They will avoid pitfalls and mistakes that the average person would blindly encounter. Those who love Him will experience favor that money would not be sufficient to cover. No amount of wealth could provide the health that often accrues from divine providence.

If money could purchase health, the founder of Apple Computers would undoubtedly be alive today. There are limits to what wealth in overcoming certain diseases, and Steve Jobs is a prominent example.

Lately, I have sounded like a scratched record that keeps repeating, "you can't make this stuff up." I discovered that when I share experiences with others, I figure out where another piece of my puzzle fits into its proper place. That's the beauty of sharing our testimonies with others going through similar experiences. We can help each other because we have been down a similar street.

Sharing personal testimonies helps us see the bigger picture and put our pieces in perspective. The benefits of sharing are by divine design. Our lives are one of many being put together. Our life cycle is only a piece of a much larger puzzle that encompasses all those who share in our world throughout our lifetime.

God created an orderly world where the pieces fit together and work properly when we trust Him to be God and submit to being His people. Although traveling through life is puzzling at times, the entire journey is well-known to God. He knows the end from the beginning and all that is in between. Nothing about us is a mystery to Him. Jeremiah was well known before he was formed, and still unknown to his parents. Those who put faith in God can trust Him to fit the pieces in their proper place in His time. When the stuff that makes up life unfolds, we realize that the happenings are something we can't fabricate. Every piece is designed to keep us looking up in expectation for what is coming next.

The narrative of the patriot, Joseph is an excellent example of puzzle pieces coming together to make sense of God's purpose. (Gen 37-50). Through his mistakes, his brothers' attempt to eliminate him, false accusations, and imprisonment, he was seemingly forgotten. Yet, in the end, the pieces of His puzzle fit where God intended. Joseph's summary to his brothers is also the answer to how God fixes our problems:

> *But as for you, you meant evil against me; but God meant it for good, in order to bring it about as it is this day, to save many people alive.* (Gen 50:20 NKJV)

For Joseph, the critical expression throughout the years of tribulations was *"The Lord was with Him"* (Gen 39:3, 21, 23). When the Lord is with those who are in a covenant relationship with Him, our lives are like that puzzle, slowly but surely being put together. It does not matter what occurs because the Lord is at work. Things will happen that leave us in awe. But, because we are in a covenant relationship with the Lord, whatever occurs may begin as a puzzle, but once the pieces are in place, the result will be good.

Today, salvation from sin—a covenant relationship with the Lord—is available for those who believe in Jesus. His final words before ascending to heaven are recorded in Matthew 28:20 "… and lo, I am with you always, *even* to the end of the age," Amen.

Believers can be like Moses, receiving commands on a mountain (Ex 19), or like David, being disciplined in the valley of the shadow of death (Ps 23). Our puzzling life keeps coming together, and the strange stuff brings us closer to the well-known purpose of our creator, who loves us. **"These are miracles you can't make up.**

Stuff we can't make up reveals Him in ways that keep us looking up beyond the hills to the Most High, who knows all things and works all things according to His divine purpose and pleasure.

Those who love Him reap the benefits that come from walking by Faith in God and not by their sight: stuff that is clearly outside of the realm of a mere accident or coincidence is a matter of divine providence, protection, and provision. This book chronicles the unthinkable things God has done to order my steps and lead me in the path of righteousness for His name's sake. Even when that path sometimes goes through the valley of the shadow of death, God can do the unthinkable for those who love Him: stuff that cannot be made up is designed to keep us looking up.

Now to Him who is able to do exceedingly abundantly above all that we ask or think, according to the power that works in us. (Eph 3:20)

Two accounts occurred before my years of ministry. The first, from my childhood, tells how I went from stuttering to perfect uttering in one day. The second chronicles my divine call to the ministry. The rest of this book is about events that occurred over 36-plus years of leadership ministry. These are testimonies of how the Lord intervened to provide *Divine Protection, Divine Providence, and Divine Provision.*

And they overcame him by the blood of the Lamb and by the word of their testimony, and they did not love their lives to the death. (Rev 12:11)

ONE SYLLABLE AWAY FROM A STUTTER

As far back as I can remember, I was a chronic stutterer. The only thing I could do was sing a song all the way through. I was about seven when my brothers and I sang at Henry Grove Missionary Baptist Church. I led a song about Noah and the ark. After the service, an elderly lady approached me and asked me my name. I began to stutter and was never able to get it out. She finally interrupted me and said, "boy, you are going to be a preacher." I never thought about it again until I eventually accepted the divine call to be a preacher.

My stuttering was so bad that my parents tried everything to get me some help. They took me to the doctors and a speech therapist. They tried various questionable remedies. "Hit him in the mouth with a dish rag while he is stuttering" is one I remember vividly. Academically, I was on point, but stuttering contributed to shaping my introverted personality.

I was in the seventh grade when the seventh and eighth-grade teachers decided to come together and do a play about Tom Sawyer. In the play, he manipulated his friends into doing his work, and convinced them to give him their snacks and belongings for the opportunity to help whitewash a fence.

As the lead, the character of Sawyer did most of the talking. And the teachers decided to give me that role to me. I was so afraid and angry at the teachers and felt they were setting me up to be humiliated by the other students.

My family raised chickens and other livestock. Seeing biddies hatch from eggs was awesome. That day, I felt like the two teachers had been hatched like biddies and not born like humans. I was so afraid! I remember saying something in my mind that I often heard my mother mumble: "Lord help me!"

I grew up with eight siblings, and cussing was forbidden. Anytime we felt like saying what was called a bad word, a holy word replaced it. We could not even say the word lie. Even as an adult, for a long time, I felt uncomfortable using the word "lie." So "Lord help me" was the safest thing I could say, though I never thought that the Lord would help me.

It was a very long play, so I began to study my part. I studied and I studied until I had memorized all of it. I knew what I was supposed to say and remembered what others were supposed to say. Even though I memorized the play very well, the fear of performance was indescribable. Growing up with a stutter was challenging. Something as simple as approaching the teacher to ask a question brought on anxiety. My speech was always a source of ridicule, with classmates laughing and making fun of me.

The dreaded day finally came. The stage was set, and the props were in place. The time came, and I watched as the seventh and eighth-grade students entered the auditorium. They were excited and anticipating a day off from regular classes. But I wish that I had never been born.

The play finally began. My fear of stuttering made me feel this was probably the day that my speech would go down as the biggest joke in Lilesville Middle School's post-segregation history.

Instead, a fantastic thing happened! I opened my mouth and, for the first time, spoke an entire sentence without stuttering. In a moment, I went from stuttering to perfect uttering! I knew the parts so well that when Mitch Lahorn forgot his line, I whispered it to him (without stuttering) so that I could then say my part. Throughout the entire play, I continued to speak without stuttering.

When I showed slight signs of stuttering, it enhanced the drama. The laughter at those times was part of making the play a big hit.

The teachers were so pleased and proud of my performance that they wanted to hold a special assembly and asked the principal if we could redo the play in front of the middle school. He agreed, and the following week, the stage was set, and the auditorium was filled. The fifth to eighth-grade students waited in anticipation. For the second time, I did most of the talking for the entire play, doing, and not once did I stutter.

That was over fifty years ago, and I have been talking ever since. It was a miracle that somehow these two teachers contributed to this significant turning point in my life. Somehow, they knew that giving me the lead role was the right thing to do.

This occurred during the early days of school integration, so much was still being done to suggest that black students were inferior to white students. That day, a black male student had the lead role in a play that required substantial memorization and mental creativity. What a mighty God we serve! You cannot make this stuff up,

God's unscripted hand in the impossible"

I am convinced the Lord used those teachers to turn my —and that of many others. In retrospect, I realize how critical the moment was. The two teachers used me to send a subtle message that black students could compete with white students. Being a male made it even more impressive.

Even today, I am keenly aware of a time when I could not say my name without stuttering. At the Bible college where I occasionally teach, students have asked me how I know what I know and minister seemingly with ease. My response is always the same. Whether teaching a class of ten students or ministering in front of thousands at an International Convention, I am always aware that I am one syllable away from a stutter. What made the difference was one day, the divine providence of God protected my mental stability and provided the healing that I needed. Just knowing I am one syllable away from a stutter contributes to my humility. God exalted me those two days of play-acting, and I am still singing: "Jesus, I'll never forget what you have done for me."

> *Pride goes before destruction, And a haughty spirit before a fall.* (Prov 16:18)

> *Humble yourselves therefore under the mighty hand of God, that he may exalt you in due time.* (1 Ptr 5:6)

THE DIVINE CALL TO THE MINISTRY

From at least the sixth grade, I was intrigued with everything electrical. Today, my siblings won't let me forget the Christmas Eve that I blew out the power trying to fix an appliance. As a kid, I always wanted the latest gadgets. That fascination led me to relocate to New Jersey to work for Bell Laboratories, which was the ultimate place to be. Once my daughter's eleventh-grade class was discussing Bell Laboratories and inventions. She said, "my daddy used to work there." Her teacher thought she was lying and told her so in front of the class. She did not talk about the incident until years after she graduated. Had I known, I would have made a trip to the school to correct him. However, this type of reputation was unique to Bell Labs. Working for Bell Labs was the ultimate career move, and I spent the remainder of my engineering career working there.

My first apartment was on the third floor of a home in Plainfield, New Jersey. Several houses in New Jersey have three floors and a basement. Each floor was like its own separate house. Although the third floor was much smaller, it was an ideal starter residence.

While asleep one night, I had an unusual dream that was like a vision in many ways. I was pinned to my bed and could hardly breathe. I attributed this to difficulty sleeping on my back. However, while struggling to breathe, I heard a voice say, "preach my word. You preach my word." Then I saw myself in the pulpit of Islen Community Church preaching extremely hard. I awoke to find myself sweating and exhausted as if I had preached.

This seemed weird, so I chalked the dream up to something I had eaten. After all, adjusting to the new diet in Jersey took some time. I hadn't had bagels before, or roast beef the way people cooked it in New Jersey. So, I brushed the intense dream off as related to something I ate. This incident occurred on a Wednesday night. The next night, it happened again just as before. This time, however, thought I didn't think deeply about it, the episode got my attention for a moment.

Then something else began to occur. Typically, our Sunday night services started with a testimony service. I'm sure that some reading this remember the Sunday night testimony services. On those nights, I would testify like everyone else. However, after the dream-vision phenomenon, I would start testifying, but end up exhorting from Scripture. This was uncomfortable because I never wanted to be out of order or seem to be trying to be something I was not.

My childhood stuttering induced me to keep a low profile so no one would notice me or call on me. An introvert will tell you that drawing attention to ourselves takes us out of our comfort zone! I love people, but can spend weeks and never see anyone. So to avoid suspicion about what might be happening, I stopped testifying.

About six months after being told to preach and then preaching in my sleep, something pressured me into submission. I was on my way to the Sunday six p.m. youth service. I wasn't running late, so I had no reason to speed in my red Honda Civic with a small motor that I called a lawnmower motor.

As I approached the top of a hill, a large U-Haul truck came into my lane. It could not have been any more than 30 feet away, but miraculously, I ended up in the ditch. It happened so fast, and I was sitting in the car in the ditch, frightened and shocked. I could see the truck that had come at me and passed by me without hitting me in my rear-view mirror.

Out of nowhere, a voice spoke within my spirit and said, "you are in my hands!" That's all the voice said. I knew it was not my imagination, but as the voice was speaking, my stress level was off the charts.

I arrived at church in tears and feeling like my world was turned upside down. I went to my pastor's office and asked if I could talk to Him. Through my tears, I told him about the ministry call that had continued to haunt me since those two dreams.

"I am supposed to be preaching," When he leaned back in his chair, and said, "I was wondering how long you were going to hold out before coming to me," I was relieved to know that I was not losing my mind. The Lord had already revealed my call to him, but he was waiting for me to step forward and accept it. However, it took God's providence that protected me from a head-on collision to bring me into submission to His will. This is stuff that I could not make up, but one of the reasons I continue to look up.

DIVINE PROTECTION

protection prə-ˈtek-shən:
The act of protecting: supervision or support of one
that is smaller and weaker.

NOT YOUR TIME TO DIE

I will never forget anything about that Christmas day, 1999. I had a deadly kidney infection, but had no idea what I was experiencing.

Earlier that season, a deacon at our church who was a mechanic told me about an associate who went home not feeling well one day and a few days later, died from a nasty kidney infection. Around the same time, I had not been feeling well, but thought I was developing a cold. So, I immediately started taking over-the-counter remedies and increased my vitamin C intake. The closer it got to Christmas Day, the more symptoms emerged. I would feel pain around my waist and in my back.

Since I had never had the flu, I had never taken the flu shot. However, I knew people who had the virus, and seemed to becoming down with that virus, so I started taking Theraflu, hoping to slow it down or stop it.

On Christmas morning, we prepared to go to my parents' home to spend the day with the family. My wife and I had agreed that we would alternate where we spent the Christmas holiday. One year we would spend it in New Jersey with her family, and the next in North

Carolina with my family. This year was the year for us to spend Christmas Day with my family. On Christmas morning, I was feeling awful. The house was warm, but I had chills, so I kept my coat on. I asked my wife and children if they were cold. They said no. Nothing I put on took away the chills. I suspected I had a fever because, though I had chills, my body felt warm.

My wife drove one hour to my parents' home since I felt terrible. By the time I reached their house, all I wanted to do was lie down. I greeted everyone and went straight to what was my old room. An hour later, when my wife came to check on me my she could squeeze water out of soaking wet clothes. Nothing that I was taking the entire day would cause my temperature to go down, so she knew something was wrong. She said, that's it; I'm taking you to the doctor. Christmas was on a Saturday. She took me to the doctor, who diagnosed me with a kidney infection. At the time, my temperature was rising to 102 -103. The doctor gave me some antibiotics and sent me home.

The next day, as time approached for church, I was still in bed. When my wife came close to me, she reached down to wake me. Before she touched me, she felt the heat from my body. Again, I was drenched, cold, and shaking. She called the doctor's office and described it all. They told her to take me to the emergency room immediately. When I arrived, my temperature was 105 degrees and rising. So they put me on an IV, trying to lower my temperature. When my temperature refused to go any lower than 105, the doctor told us I had the worst kidney infection he had ever seen!

I remembered that a few days earlier, I had heard that someone had died from a kidney infection. He told us that the high temperature had been a blessing in that it prevented the infection from moving out of my kidneys. If it had dropped, the infection would have gone straight to my heart and instantly killed me!" What he described as luck was undeniably divine protection. God refused to let me die! He did it again. This was one of those stories you cannot make!

I was hospitalized for an entire week so they could work on the infection and restore my temperature. Some days it would drop to 102 but rise back to 105. It got so consistent that I knew my temperature based on how I felt. It wasn't four days later that my body began to return to normal. By that Friday, my temperature was normal. I went home on Saturday morning. To God be the glory!

Since then, I've discovered that kidney infections are more common during the holiday season. Yet, episodes such as this convince me that no one checks out of this world without God signing off on it. I survived an infection that caused many others to lose their lives. My unchanging temperature was part of a divine plan.

I will praise You, for I am fearfully and wonderfully made; Marvelous are Your works, And that my soul knows very well. My frame was not hidden from You,

When I was made in secret, And skillfully wrought in the lowest parts of the earth. (Ps 139:14-15)

Until that time, my favorite soda was Mountain Dew, and I probably consumed at least one or two every week. But, since then, I have stopped drinking because after I was released from the hospital, I knew I had to change my behavior and began drinking more water. I do not take the mercy the Lord had mercy lightly, and will not tempt the Lord my God (Matt 4:7). When I was ignorant of the importance of drinking water, rather than sodas, God spared my life and my loved ones from tears because it was not my time to die! The Psalmist sums up my feelings about those two weeks when I would not die.:

I shall not die, but live, And declare the works of the LORD. The LORD has chastened me severely, But He has not given me over to death. Open to me the gates of righteousness; I will go through them, And I will praise the LORD. (Ps 118:17-19)

WHAT DO YOU MEAN INTENSIVE CARE?

My oldest daughter came home one day not feeling well, which wasn't unusual for a middle schooler, nor the first time she came home feeling ill. So, as before, her mother told her to lie down for a while. However, this usual instruction could have become an unusual tragedy.

When Doctor G came to pick up her son, my daughter left her room and lay down on the floor at the beginning of the Hall. When Doctor G walked through the door and was preparing her son to leave, she looked over, saw my daughter, and asked what was wrong with her. We told her that she wasn't feeling well, so we told her to go and lie down. Doctor G, I assumed, was doing what would be an automatic response for a doctor. She started to walk towards my daughter. Before going any further, I need to rewind and explain how my wife became the babysitter for Doctor G's then-infant child.

The sister of a member of our church lived in Indiana, but knew that G in Charlotte, North Carolina, was looking for a babysitter so she could return to her medical practice. They were looking for a babysitter with specific requirements that grossly limited their list of choices for caring for their infant son.

The sister from Indiana called her sister in Charlotte to see if anyone from my church would fit the bill. She asked my wife if she would be interested in keeping the baby for a few years, and she agreed. Since both were doctors, one parent would bring him in the morning, and his mother would generally pick him up in the evening.

On that day, when our world seemed to abruptly turn upside down. Doctor G inquired about my daughter, who had crawled out of bed and was lying on the floor at the end of the hall. As Doctor G leaned over and touched my daughter's chest, what she did would forever be etched in my mind! She picked her up quickly, ran to the door with her in her arms, and told us to follow her in our car, put my daughter in her car, and sped off. We were doing everything to keep up with Doctor G, who had put on her blinkers. I do not remember if either of us ran red lights, for it happened so fast.

We had no clue where Doctor G was going or why she was going so fast to get there. We were afraid and nearly in shock, so we did not talk in the car. As we went down the highway and began to turn, I realized that Doctor G was speeding toward the Presbyterian hospital. She pulled into the emergency entrance, jumped out of the car, scooped up our daughter, and ran into the emergency room. By the time I walked through the door, Doctor G was hooking my daughter up with all types of tubes, screaming out instructions to nurses, and had the entire room in full emergency mode. I was clueless as to what was going on, but knew that whatever was occurring was extremely serious.

My daughter ended up in intensive care for the night and the next day. Much later, when we finally got to talk to Doctor G, what she told us left me stunned and nearly in shock! Doctor G said that she barely breathed when she touched our daughter's chest. "Her breathing was equivalent to someone trying to breathe through a straw." She noted that her breathing was so faint that it was moments from stopping altogether. She was afraid and knew that time was

> **Her breathing was equivalent to someone trying to breathe through a straw.**

not on our side. So, she acted swiftly, not knowing if she would lose her before reaching the hospital. As it turned out, her diagnosis was a severe bronchial attack with her windpipe nearly wholly closed. She was in a daze and thinking about the amazing God we serve, who did not allow our firstborn to die in her sleep. Also, she said it was good that she did not stay in bed but crawled up the hall where we could see her. Dr. G was convinced that "she would not have made it through the night."

So many years later, I am fighting back the tears as I recall the day when Doctor G came out of the emergency room and said to us," She is in intensive care, and we will have to monitor her throughout the night." She said, "At this time, that is all we can say, but I know she had a terrible bronchial attack."

As she gave the dismal diagnosis, my mind was stuck on the words "Intensive care." I remember thinking, "Intensive care, what do you mean intensive care?" Eventually, our daughter recovered and was taken out of intensive care, and she never had another episode like it.

The pieces of this puzzling incident fit together perfectly to save my daughter's life. A member of our church in Charlotte had a sister in Indiana who knew a doctor in Charlotte who was looking for a babysitter. The member contacted my wife, who agreed to take on the task, even though she had four pre-adolescent children. No more than six months later, this doctor came to pick up her child, and because my daughter happened to crawl out of bed, the doctor saw her in distress on the floor.

Because Doctor G was in our house that day, our daughter's life was saved.

The sequence of events that put a medical doctor in my house when my daughter was silently fighting for her life is nothing less than incredible! The intervention was solely an act of God looking out for us, even when we had no clue that we needed Him to do so. If you had a thousand years to try, you could not make this stuff up.

What are the chances that these pieces would fit so perfectly in place to save the life of my daughter without divine intervention? Being young parents who had put her to bed for rest, it would have been unbearable had she died in her sleep that night, and we discovered, when it was too late, that putting her to bed was a fatal and costly mistake.

What does intensive care mean? My daughter was receiving intensive care when God put the right people in the right place before her parents put her in the wrong place—her bed. This incident is beyond our ability to conjure up. To God be the glory for the things that he has done! I can say, as Israel said when the LORD turned the captivity of Zion again:

> *The LORD hath done great things for us; whereof we are glad* (Ps 126:3

I AM GOING TO BURN THEM UP

I am writing this on one of the coldest mornings that the nation has experienced, especially in the South.

However, I remember one of the coldest nights in the late eighties, when we were living in a home that made use of a heat pump. It seemed to reach its maximum capacity on this night and was of little help. I learned later that the appliances tend not to work when temperatures drop below a threshold number. And this was one of those nights.

Our two girls and two boys had separate bedrooms. But, since the heat pump was not functioning properly, we set them up in the boys' bedroom and used a space heater to supplement the inadequate heating. The room had bunk beds, making it a better option. As the temperature continued to drop on that frigid night, I turned the control button of the heater to the highest setting to quickly warm the room.

Shortly after 10 p.m. and their bedroom was diagonally across from our bedroom. Shortly

After putting them to bed, my wife and I retired for the night, sat up in bed, and watched television while she was sewing. I soon fell asleep and either had a dream or a vision; it was hard to tell. I saw a figure at the bottom of my bed, saying to me, "I am going to burn them up, and you can't do anything about it! In the air, I could see the children's bedroom on fire. The blaze was in the air. As I slept and saw their burning room in my sleep, I struggled to say, Jesus. When I tried to say, Jesus, it was as if something was stopping my speech. The best I could get from my lips was a "Je" sound. I struggled until I finally could say, Jesus!

Then I jumped up. I told my wife, if you ever see me grappling in my sleep that way, shake me and say Jesus to wake me up.

I quickly got out of bed and ran toward the children's room. As soon as I open the door, the heat hits me in the face. I ran over and unplugged the space heater. The insulation on it was already starting to melt, and the heater was minutes away from setting the room on fire.

I cannot explain what the figure was in my sleep. However, whatever it was, it tipped me off and caused me to wake up and stop the room from catching fire. To God be the glory!

LIFE SPARED GOD CARES

About a month before writing this account, I heard of a fatal head-on collision on the highway north of our house. A car ended up going the wrong way in traffic, and several people lost their lives. The accident took me back to several years earlier when my wife and I could have met a similar fate.

Late one Friday night, we had just finished a Friday night marriage and counseling seminar in a church in rural Virginia. We had an excellent seminar session that was so intense that it lasted longer than anticipated. Everyone appeared excited about what was yet to come the next morning.

It was late, so we went outside, and some church members followed us to our car. We looked forward to going to the hotel to get a good night's rest so we could get an early start for the second day of the seminar.

We pulled out of the church's parking lot and headed down the street, but were unknowingly traveling the wrong way. We saw people waving their hands and arms, but thought they were waving us off. Rather, they were trying to stop us because we did not go far enough. There were no streetlights, and the large trees hanging over made it very dark, so we could not see a grass divider, or that beyond that divider were the lanes we were supposed to turn onto to go right. Since we saw two lanes, we turned onto the outside lane and headed down the street. But we were on the wrong side, going the wrong way. We were supposed to have turned right and gone a few hundred feet to a divider that would have allowed us to cross the median onto the right lanes of the highway.

Later, the people outside told us that they were waving and screaming, trying to flag us down, but we did not stop. As our car faded out of sight, they went back into the church and started praying. They were afraid and feared the worst, which appeared to be inevitable. As my wife and I drove along, talking about the night we had experienced, the lights of at least two cars blinked and passed by on the left. For me, blinking lights were a warning that a police car was ahead. Shortly, a car came straight at me and started blowing its horn. I swerved a little to the right and barely missed the car. I remember saying, "um, that car was coming straight at me," but was still clueless that I was on the wrong side of the road.

Then a car with flashing blue lights came at me and maneuvered me off the road. I knew that it was a police car. After forcing me off the road, he went a little further, crossed the median, and quickly came back in front of me with his blue lights now turned on. I wasn't speeding, and all my lights were working, so I began to pull out my registration as he got out of his car and came toward us.

A policeman comes straight at us to force us off the road.

This was before the 2016 elections and before there was an escalation in people of color being shot in traffic accidents. So, I had no reason to fear for our lives at the time. He came to the car and asked if I had been drinking. I said no. There was an urgency in his voice as he spoke. As he asked for my license and registration, he told me I was on the wrong side of the road and that he forced me off the highway because beyond that hill, both lanes were full of traffic that included 18-wheelers coming our way. While he was speaking, the heavy traffic began to top the hill and pass us. He had forced me about half a mile from the incline where no car lights could be seen until one was close to topping the hill.

Usually, street traffic slows down when a police car is on the road, and no one wants to pass the police car. However, that night it was as if he were leading a funeral procession, and no one wanted to pass him. Because he was on the road, the traffic was delayed, and built up behind him instead of reaching our car. He told us that he had gone to Richmond to drop off an inmate and was returning home to Lynchburg, and decided to take the back road. Because of this, he was in place to protect us from what would have been a certain head-on collision and a multiple-car accident with multiple fatalities. If he were not a state trooper, he was a divine trooper and a divine messenger. God placed him on the road to save our lives because our ministry was not done. The Lord Jesus had more for us to complete.

The trooper was agitated but friendly and showed great concern for us. He did not give me a ticket, but stayed with us with the blue lights on as the heavy traffic that had backed up passed us. When the traffic thinned out, he helped us to get on the right side of the road without risking running into more traffic that was now running at the 65 mph speed limit.

We left the scene praising and thanking God for again protecting us and sparing our lives. But it wasn't until around 3 a.m. in the morning, that what had occurred sunk into my spirit. At that time, I found myself thanking God in tears. My wife and I shed tears together, thinking about what could have been.

When we showed up at church the next day, everyone was so glad to see us! They were concerned about what had happened to us. They said that after they could not stop us, they went back into the church, went on their knees, and began praying for us. Some said they even turned on the Television to watch the late-night news to see if a bad accident was reported.

My wife and I talked about how a tragic accident would have been too much for anyone in our world to bear. It would have been hard for the church that invited us, our children, the church family, and the organizational family. We could only shake our heads, thinking about how God cares for us. We were so awed that we did not know how to thank God for what he had done. To say we were speechless puts it too lightly. It seemed as though anything we tried to do to say thank you would not have been enough. God unscripted and miraculously intervened. Saying anything else felt so inadequate for our souls being delivered from death. As the Psalmist, we could only vow:

For You have delivered my soul from death, my eyes from tears, And my feet from falling. I will walk before the LORD in the land of the living. (Ps 116:8)

Walking before the Lord according to His written word is the one thing we can do. In protecting us, our God spared those who loved us the pain of such a loss. Our Lord spared us because he cared about us. Sparing our lives does not suggest that God did not care about those who lost their lives on that interstate. My spirit sank within me when I heard the news. I believe it was their time to leave this earth, so God signed off on their transition, for no one checks out of this world without God signing off on it. Because it was not our time, the Lord had our angel in place to assure that what could have been a fatality did not occur.

Are not all angels ministering spirits sent to serve those who will inherit salvation? (Heb 1:14)

I am conscious of this truth that when we are heirs of salvation, those we encounter help keep us safe even when we do not know that we are in danger. Because as heirs, we have angels that serve us, situations will arise that cause us to say: "You cannot make this stuff up. Only God Could Do This."

I speak to all heirs of salvation. We each have at least one angel assigned to serve us. I do not doubt that our angels served us well that night. Only God knows if the man who forced us off the road was one of our angels. Therefore, I literally live by the exhortations in Psalms and Hebrews:

The angel of the LORD encampeth round about them that fear him, and delivereth them. (Ps 34:7)

Keep on loving one another as brothers and sisters. Do not forget to show hospitality to strangers, for by so doing some people have shown hospitality to angels without knowing it. (Heb 13:1-2)

GOING TO KILL THE FIRST PERSON

In the early days of my pastoral ministry, Tuesday evenings were set aside as the designated time for prayer around the altar. On this particular night, we had just gathered and were standing together, preparing to share our prayer requests before kneeling for the hour of prayer.

A man who appeared to have been drinking pushed the door open and stood at the back. From my vantage point, I wasn't quite sure. He interrupted us with a loud question, "Who is in charge?" When I responded that I was the pastor, he said he wanted to talk to me. So, I took him to a small room near the entrance.

He asked me to pray for him. And as I ended my prayer and opened my eyes, he stuck his hand into his pants and pulled a knife out of his pants that looked exactly like a soldier's knife. It happened so fast that I did not have time to think about what he would do with the knife.

When it was entirely out of his pants, he raised it and handed it to me. I reached out my arms, and he laid it in my hand. Then he said, "I left home to kill the first person who said something bad. But when I passed by this door, something told me to go inside and see the man." The man he came to see was me.

He had been drinking and drugging, but was in a lot of mental and emotional pain. I did the only thing I knew how to do: I offered to baptize him in the name of Jesus. He agreed, but since we did not have a pool in our church, we had to travel forty-five minutes to Troutman, North Carolina, to baptize Him in our Bishop's baptismal pool. I had never seen the man before, so we were still trying to err on the side of caution. Someone drove while he and I sat in the back of the car. I baptized him in the name of Jesus; what occurred next was phenomenal for me. The man who had lain on my shoulder to Troutman, intoxicated, was now sober and able to speak coherently as we returned to Charlotte.

On the entire trip to Troutman, he lay his head on my shoulder, and for about two weeks after this, that shoulder was extremely sore. It felt like a heavy weight had been put on it, and it was injured. At times, it felt like it was broken. I felt sad for him as he lay on my shoulder. But in the end, though he felt hopeless, he was miraculously protected from making a mistake that could have cost him his freedom. I was miraculously saved from his vengeance because I was the first person he saw. But rather than saying something terrible to him, He heard about Jesus, who was good for him. To God be the glory for divine protection!

Who Himself bore our sins in His own body on the tree, that we, having died to sins, might live for righteousness-- by whose stripes you were healed (1 Ptr 2:24)

DIVINE PROVIDENCE

providence ˈprä-və-dən(t)s :
Divine guidance or care

IS IT TOO HARD FOR GOD?

Before becoming a full-time pastor, I worked at Computer of the Carolinas, which later merged with PC Mart. Since the church needed all the funds that were coming in to maintain it, everything that came in supported the ministry. Occasionally, I would receive a stipend, but the church never went lacking. Besides, God had blessed me with a talent that He enabled me to perfect.

There are very few things I hate worse than secondhand cigarette smoke, and before smoking was outlawed in closed places, since there were several smokers in my place of employment, at times, my clothes would smell like cigarette smoke when I got to church. — The smell would get in my clothes and linger, to be on time. I often went straight from work to church; I did not have time to go home and change. I was self-conscious and concerned that someone would conclude that "the pastor was a smoker."

I remember praying and asking the Lord to get me into a smoke-free environment. One night, I dreamed that a hurricane came through and destroyed the building where I was employed. In the dream, I ran through the door, and the place was heavily damaged, but no one was there but me. I ran into the back where my office was located and found no one. So, I walked back out into the large display area. As I stood there, I looked out of the large glass windows in the front of the store facing the street. Suddenly, the sun began to slowly rise on the horizon beyond the storm clouds. At that moment, I woke up. I sensed that the dream was significant. I told my wife that we should probably try to save as much as possible because I might be out of a job at some point.

Approximately two years later, I left home and went straight to a client's site. As I worked on their computer, I needed some parts I did not have. I called the office to check the inventory before making a trip to the office. I dialed the number, and a message came on and said, "This number is no longer in service...." I tried it several times with the same results. I got back in my car and hurried back to the office. When I went to the door to enter, Federal Marshals were guarding the entrance. After asking me to identify myself, they told me to come in, get my personal belongings, and exit the building.

Later, I found out that the executives of PC Mart were involved in some illegal activities. The marshal seized everything in sight. We were all suddenly out of a job. People were screaming, crying, angry, and expressing mixed emotions. However, because of the dream I had two years prior, we had put away some emergency funds. The incident shocked me, but I was not distraught. The executives were planning to have an emergency meeting that night, but since it was Wednesday night, I chose to go to the midweek service and get the meeting information later. Yes, I was concerned, but I was also prepared to be without a job. Thank God for divine guidance. I wasn't sure what to do next. I thought about taking some time off and focusing on ministry. But I kept getting calls from some vendors and clients. Even Compaq computers, a popular computer manufacturer at the time, was trying to convince me to relocate to Atlanta and work in a corporate office. By this time, the ministry was a priority, so leaving Charlotte was not an option.

In the past, I had contemplated branching out on my own and consulting. However, I could never get up the courage to go from a guaranteed paycheck to having to pay myself. During this time, I remembered my prayer to be delivered from a smoke-filled cigarette environment. I remember saying after the closure, "Lord, I wanted out, but I did not mean for you to shut this place down. Now I am out of a job!" At the time, I thought God needed me to point this out to Him.

It was going into the summer, and I had installed several multiuser multitasking computers to run accounting departments. I was a Unix (Xenix) specialist. Simply stated, finding someone to repair the Altos computers and maintain the operating systems was not easy. Also, the Altos computers had ports susceptible to electrical spikes. That summer, it seemed like an electrical storm was occurring every week, and the Altos computers were failing everywhere. I worked as much out of a job as I did while working at PC Mart, but the money was coming to me. I remember thinking this may be the time for me to enter a full-time business. It would afford me the flexibility to continue my theological education. But when I thought about being the sole provider for my wife and four small children, I was not willing to launch into those deep waters.

I remembered the biblical examples of the fleece (Judg. 6:37-38), but I did not take it seriously. But I was not sure if God was saying that my prayer had been answered, for that would have been getting a better job in a smoke-free environment. Instead, I had the employment rug pulled from under me. Yes, I had preached that things could

> **I thought I was giving God something that He would not do.**

get worse in God before they get better, but that was for my congregation, not for me. Here I was forced to practice the faith I had been teaching and preaching.

Since I was still too afraid to go out on my own, I found something hard and seemingly impossible and put it before God. I had not contacted the client whom I helped for anything since the initial installation and warranty period. I said, "Lord, if you are telling me to go out on my own, I'll know it if 'Kale Office Outfitters' calls me." They were located on the service road off Interstate 85. I knew they would not contact me, especially since PC Mart was no longer there. They had a computer-savvy office manager and had already stopped calling me. No phone call would confirm that God was not directing me to go into my own business. This was my Gideon fleece. I was thinking this was the right thing for a disciple of Jesus to do, but I was far from being sure. I had nothing to lose, for I was out of a permanent job.

As I look back on the experience, I was trying to find a way out of being self-employed. My family and bills needed me to have a guaranteed amount each week. My resume was already getting some activity. But I could not ignore those opportunities to make money while I was not employed. My tithes, offerings, and bills continued to be paid. I knew God was at work, but I wasn't sure that this was how I wanted Him to work it out for me. I was praying hard, but it was not an *on-my-knees prayer*. I was having a mental conversation with God about a hard thing that I did not expect to happen, and its not happening would help God understand my position. I would then feel justified in interviewing and taking the best-paying job with the benefits I needed to sustain a young family.

Two days after I put this test before God, I received a phone call around 6 AM. This person with a very country voice said, "Is this Ron that used to work at PC Mart?" I said yes. She replied This is JT, office manager at Kale Office Outfitters, and we have been looking for you. Can you make a service call? We will pay you!

Believe me when I say I did not know whether to be extremely scared or shocked!

There is not enough space in this book to share all the blessings and benefits of that decision. I did this until the Lord told me to come off my job. The rest is His-story. The puzzle of my life keeps being put together by my Lord. Thank You, Jesus.

When I say you can't make this stuff up, I mean Only God Could Do This! But these situations keep many Christians, including me, looking up in expectation for the next great move of God that climaxes in the return of Christ! *"For yet a little while, And He who is coming will come and will not tarry (*Hebrews 10:37).

> *Trust in the LORD with all your heart And lean not on your own understanding; In all your ways acknowledge Him, And He shall direct your paths.* (Prov 3:5-6)

Not As I Will But As You Will

I'm often asked if pastoring a church was my reason for relocating to Charlotte, North Carolina, after living in New Jersey for several years. The answer is an emphatic no! After spending several years in New Jersey working at Bell Laboratories and attending the Islen Community Church, I decided to relocate back to North Carolina. I enjoyed where I worked, and the church I attended was second to none, but the cold weather drove me back south.

One winter, I had to get on top of my completely covered little Honda Civic and dig it out of the snow. I remember thinking, "This is for the birds." I probably should have said, "This is not even for the birds," because even they journey south to avoid the winter cold. So, moving back south had to do with my dislike of the bitterly cold winters that seemed to last through springtime.

I had made no plans, and I do mean no plans, for a church affiliation, and had not considered pastoring a church. Though I've been pastoring for nearly 40 years, the journey did not begin with my willingness to pastor. Initially, I refused to return to the place I first visited. At the time, it was called the "Living Church of Jesus" and was where the Bishop of the Diocese held meetings in Charlotte. His primary place of worship was in another city. He kept this church open as a commitment to a deceased ministry acquaintance, but the only members were from two small families, and I decided this was not for me! Let me explain why.

Once I settled in the south, I looked up the name of the Bishop in the Church of Our Lord Jesus Christ (COOLJC) in my area of North Carolina. I found him at a diocese meeting held in Raleigh, North Carolina. Later, I visited the place in Charlotte where the recently appointed Bishop of the Diocese had stepped in to help this small family. Before his death, their father was the pastor. Although fewer than five people, they were committed to continuing the ministry. When I walked in the door this Sunday morning, the Bishop and the deceased pastor's teenage son were warming themselves at a kerosene heater in the middle of the floor. I remember thinking that this was 1985, and I did not know that anyone was still doing the 1920s thing with a kerosene heater. By today's standards, their little building should have been condemned as uninhabitable.

I was cordial, but I had decided that I was not coming back, and it would be the only time I would be in that building. I was convinced that it was a shack and no one should be in it doing anything! I certainly was not going to attend church at this place. My church in New Jersey was quite different and what I had become accustomed to for corporate worship. At the time, I did not consider that for the bishop and the young man, it was a time of recovery for continuation. I was only thinking about what I desired as a place of worship for my family and myself.

So I am seeking an alternative place to take my little family for worship.

What happened on a Friday night about a month later changed the trajectory of my life forever. Before mentioning what happened, I must rewind to my days at Bell Laboratories. There, we had clubs and activities designed to keep us working closely. In the winter, we had intramural basketball tournaments. One Friday night, I scored 51 points while playing. I could not believe how it seemed I could not miss a shot. I had never done this before, and never did it again. But I injured my knee, and I continued to play. I never recovered from the injury. I was not in constant pain. Yet though it did not last long, it periodically gave out on me, and I would fall. Now, back to Friday night in North Carolina.

I had just finished taking a shower. I stepped out of the bathtub and must have twisted my knee. This time, I fell to the floor and could not get back up. Only my oldest daughter was home with me. I remember being in much pain as I tried to crawl to the bedroom. Seemingly out of nowhere, I heard an internal, inaudible voice that softly said, "Now find Bishop W." Since I could not get up off the floor, my daughter called 911, and an ambulance took me to the emergency room.

Tests and X-rays confirmed that I had a torn cartilage in the middle of my knee. Since it was still connected on each edge, the doctors could do arthroscopic surgery and remove the torn piece. However, they did not tell me that no exercise or therapy would bring that knee back to its pre-surgery functioning. To this day, my right knee is not as strong as my left one.

That divine guidance on that dismal night caused me to reconnect with Bishop W. This was on a Friday night, and two days later, I called His House on Sunday morning. Mother W answered the phone, and I asked to speak to Bishop W. From that time forward, I humbled myself and returned to where I had refused to be found.

Returning and becoming subject to him was the beginning of what grew into a father-son relationship. He served him as an executive secretary, and we were so close that some people thought I was His biological son. He saw my potential before I knew the Lord's purpose for my life. He appointed me the pastor of the Living Church of Jesus when I was 27. After the providential encounter that left me unable to walk, I was done saying no to Bishop W! Also, at the time, I didn't know enough to say I was too young, given my small family. With all the bloopers, blunders, and pitfalls of trying to do it right, my love for God and His mercy that endures forever has made the difference in the survival and constant revival of the ministry.

Several ministers and church leaders have been birthed and trained at TLC and have become pastors and leaders. The ministry has grown to two campuses, with a Learning Academy at the Charlotte location. My philosophy of ministry is built on what drove the Apostle

Paul to put his past in the proper perspective so he could put his energy into pressing toward his ultimate future goal:

> *Not as though I had already attained, either were already perfect: but I follow after, if that I may apprehend that for which also I am apprehended of Christ Jesus.* (Phil 3:12)

The Lord stopped the Apostle Paul on the road to Damascus (Acts 9), and stopped me on the road to destruction and self-indulgence. Trying to apprehend why the Lord Jesus apprehended me now provides the "wind beneath my wings" as I continue mounting up with wings as an eagle. The knee surgery helped me decide that being rigid about what I will do is not worth the pitfalls and altar visits that this attitude creates. I learned the hard way that when a person belongs to the Lord, they don't have the privilege of saying what they will do without risking a rebuke from God. Good for me that He is a God of multiple chances.

I speak to those who know we are bought with a price and are not in charge of their destiny. The most powerful prayer to ensure our steps are guided by the Lord Jesus was the one He prayed when facing the most painful ordeal of His life. Our sins were about to be beaten into His flesh while His blood was about to be poured out of Him. The prophet Isaiah tells us that His appearance was marred more than any other person (Isa 52:14). His prayer of commitment to the will of God is recorded in the synoptic gospels, though each shares slightly different details.

> *He went a little farther and fell on His face, and prayed, saying, O My Father, if it is possible, let this cup pass from Me; nevertheless, not as I will, but as You will.* (Matt 26:39)

This type of prayer assures the child of God that they are led in the path of righteousness for His name's sake. God's sharp rebukes were never something I would have chosen or imagined, but because it happened, I now pray for the Lord's will to be done, even if it means being blocked or disappointed by Him. Each day, I have come to value the spirit of His word as the Psalmist declares,

> *Your word is a lamp to my feet And a light to my path.* (Ps 119:105)

This passage graphically speaks to me. Using the word as a lamp helps to illuminate where I am in life (purpose), and as a light, His word helps me properly navigate where I am going (destiny). The word of God helps me know if I am in the right location and whether I am traveling in the right direction.

BLESSED BY A DRUNK DEACON

In my nearly 40 years in ministry leadership, this testimony is one of the most powerful. I was blessed by a drunk man who professed to be a deacon. This encounter sent my theology into a tailspin, forcing me to rethink it. I realized that God does not have to follow our ethical

> **God can break our rules and still be His righteous self.**

rules to get His point across. He can do whatever He wants and use whomever He wants because he is God by Himself.

After God's rebuke and the knee surgery helped me get beyond self-indulgence, it humbled me. I submitted to God's will and accepted the preaching position at this location, where initially I was determined not to return. Placing me at the BF location freed the bishop to focus on His other duties. I decided that if this was where God willed me, and was determined to make the place look presentable. This became my priority.

The church was next door to a bar that saw heavy traffic on Saturday evenings, which caused an overflow of traffic into the church parking lot. Saturday afternoon was my preferred time to make the church presentable for the next day. This Saturday, I worked long and hard. It was about six thirty in the evening, and I had much more to do before I felt satisfied with how the place looked. To say that I was discouraged would be putting it lightly. I was having a pity party in my mind, which helped me hit the walls out of preparation for the next day and relieve some frustration for that present moment.

I was young, my family was young, and I was in this place doing what I was doing, knowing that I would have to get up the next day and minister to a few people apart from my small family. I felt it, but I only had to take out my frustration on myself until a man stumbled through the door.

I remember nailing on the wall and tearing away bad wall plaster. The sound must have been loud enough to be heard in the parking lot. A man who heard me was leaving the bar, but he came inside to see what I was doing. He greeted me and told me he was a deacon in a much larger church across the street from us. In retrospect, he was who I needed to blow off steam and project my disappointment onto someone else. My response to him went something like, "You ought to be ashamed of yourself! You are a deacon in the church, and you stumble in here drunk. We are a few people, but at least we are serious about what we are doing!"

The tone of my voice was one of rebuke. I felt relief rebuking him and pointed out his transgression. When I finished verbally attacking him for impious behavior, in a slurred voice, he responded, I know you are serious because ain't no young man your age going to be in this building on a Saturday evening banging on the wall unless he was serious!

After speaking those words to me, he turned and walked out the door. He was drunk, but his sober response caught me off guard and left me nearly staggering. My response was a combination of shock and amazement, but it was so encouraging that it left me speechless. When he left, I remember feeling better than I did before he entered the building. I even felt better about what I was doing and suddenly realized why I was doing it. The words from his mouth made me think differently about sacrificing a Saturday evening to prepare for a Sunday morning.

But being blessed by a drunk deacon did not fit neatly into my theology of who God uses. In my mind, God was not supposed to use a drunk man for anything, but coming to the altar to be delivered from his drunkenness. What added insult to this injury to my theology was that the drunk man said he was a deacon in the church across the street. How could a "drinking to drunkenness" deacon bless me, a sober minister who never wanted to drink anything more potent than a mountain dew? It left me baffled but feeling blessed. How does that happen without God? Only He can do it. You can't make it up.

I shared this encounter that blessed me on numerous occasions as a testimony to how I was encouraged by the words of a drunk deacon. But approximately twelve years later and several shares later, I received another revelation about what occurred that day. The Lord's providential use of a drunk deacon to bring me words of encouragement was a sharp rebuke to my thoughts as I worked in the church building. I was complaining to myself about having to spend time repairing and working in the place, while I knew that only a few people would show up the next day for service. It was in my mind that it would possibly only be myself, my wife, and three children in church the next day (my fourth and youngest son was not born at the time).

So much was happening at the time; I had no clue if anyone would show up for service the next day. This sense of uncertainty and sermon preparation time added to my frustration. I remember one Sunday, while my family and I sat waiting for others, no one showed up. I was embarrassed and ashamed to come out of the little office and face my family. But while I sat waiting, my oldest daughter, about four years old at the time, got up and picked up a tambourine, went up to the front, and started beating the tambourine and singing a song (I'm tearing up as I write this). When I heard her voice, I came out of the office, went up to the little homemade pulpit, and stepped up on the squeaking floor. I preached that day as if the church were full of listeners.

Although I had read it several times, that day I experienced the words of Jesus as he quoted from a prophetic Psalms (Ps 8:2). As He rebuked an indignant religious delegation, saying to them,

>*...Yes. Have you never read, 'Out of the mouth of babes and nursing infants You have perfected praise'?* (Matt 21:16)

Reflecting on those days, it humbles me to think that God has never allowed me to sink so low that it was impossible to rise back up. Yet he would not let me get so high that coming back down would require a fatal rebuke. The Lord Jesus heard my mumbling and complaining and summoned a drunk deacon to chastise and revive me. Yes, God sent that drunk deacon to sober up my thinking. It took years for me to fully comprehend the magnitude of what occurred that day! The understanding of the *reviving rebuke* revealed to me several years later

God sent a drunk deacon to sober up my thinking.

was that if a drunk hypocritical churchgoer could see through his drunkenness that I was serious, what does that say about God, who is constantly observing what we do?

God was building my character for what was to come. Part of a minister's character development is proving what one is willing to do for God when no one is looking or praising them. When God ordains and approves what you are doing, reaping comes, in His time, if we persevere in doing good and do not faint. As the Apostle Paul exhorts the church at Galatia,

> *let us not grow weary while doing good, for in due season we shall reap if we do not lose heart* (Gal 6:9)

Also, James encourages saints to persevere when bombarded by trials.

My brethren, count it all joy when you fall into various trials, knowing that the testing of your faith produces patience. But let patience have its perfect work, that you may be perfect and complete, lacking nothing. (Jas 1:2-4)

With all that I had going, giving up and fainting was an attractive option. I was pastoring, parenting, being a provider, being a husband, and renovating a building with little help. As I looked back, I was growing weary.

However, the early days in ministry were my proving season. They allowed faith to develop the patience for ministry leadership, which is critical for those shepherding God's people. Just as natural sheep require a patient shepherd, the sheep of the Lord's pasture require leaders with the patience that can only come from character development. What God said to Jeremiah is still true today for those who expect to lead the people of God.

And I will give you shepherds (calling) according to My heart (character), who will feed you with knowledge and understanding (competence) (Jer 3:1)

God appoints and anoints shepherds, and develops their character so that they can lead and feed His flock. However, competence develops as the shepherd takes the initiative to prepare to fulfill the call from God. If it is God's will for you to be an under-shepherd of the Chief Shepherd, do not expect to be handed a trial-free ministry that blows up overnight! As David, the model, as shepherd, tells us in Psalm 23:3, *He leads me in the paths of righteousness for His name's sake.* Note that paths are plural. Ministry development requires going down different paths. One path he identifies in the very next verse *through the valley of the shadow of death,* but yet, *I will fear no evil; For You are with me; Your rod and Your staff, they comfort me.* (Ps 23:4).

As part of my character development. I've been through the valley of the shadow of death. On several occasions, I traveled through the dismal valley where death was close enough to cast its shadow over my life. Given this unavoidable reality for those called to the ministry of the gospel, the proper response to walking the paths of righteousness is to grow in step with the Lord's leading, allowing our faith to cultivate patience—an essential quality for every disciple of Jesus Christ.

The rebuke I received from the drunk deacon put my thinking on the right track. When you are serious about God, His silence does not mean a lack of concern or inability to see and hear. Often, God's silence teaches us to trust Him no matter what. It does not matter if we are like Israel at the Red Sea with seemingly nowhere to go (Ex. 14), or like the disciples experiencing a violent storm of life (Mk. 4:38). Those who belong to the Lord must stand still to see his salvation. Perishing in the deep is impossible for those who love the Lord and are called according to His purpose.

So beloved of God, if you have ever been rebuked and encouraged by God through an unlikely medium while trying to please God, these two passages are for your encouragement.

> *Remembering without ceasing your work of faith, labor of love, and patience of hope in our Lord Jesus Christ in the sight of our God and Father, 4 knowing, beloved brethren, your election by God.* (1 Thess 1:3-4)

> *For God is not unjust to forget your work and labor of love which you have shown toward His name, in that you have ministered to the saints, and do minister.* (Heb 6:10)

PEWS IN THEM HILLS!

It was a beautiful Saturday morning and a perfect day for a family outing. We decided to take the children on an outing to Tweetsie Railroad theme Park between Boone and Blowing Rock, North Carolina, where the mountains begin to be defined. As we traveled, we were near the town of Hickory, where the flat land was becoming a small hill. As we approached Hickory, thoughts of church pews entered my mind. As with so many other needs we had for our place of ministry, pews were a constant theme in my prayers.

The closer we got to Hickory, the more I thought about pews. At the time, roadside phone booths were still around. As we traveled on Route 321, I noticed one of the booths on the side of the road. Since I could not get pews off my mind, I pulled over, went to the phone booth, and searched through the large yellow pages secured inside the booth. Since the town of Hickory was known for furniture-making factories, I figured there was probably a company that sold pews. To my surprise, my search of the phone book did not reveal a place that made and sold pews. So I got back into the car and went on to Tweetsie Railroad. We enjoyed a full day of family-oriented wild-west type amusement, and by the end of the day, the thoughts of pews and benches had faded and become a distant memory.

The following Tuesday morning, I received a phone call from a real estate agent helping us look for a better building to rent or buy for the church. I had not spoken to him for at least two years, so initially, I did not recognize his voice. He called to ask if we were still looking for pews. I said yes. He said a church is getting rid of its benches and related furniture in preparation for a complete renovation of the sanctuary. He went on to say that he thought about us and called me. I said yes, we were interested, and asked if there was a cost. He said no, and all we had to do was come and get them.

At that point, I was excited, and I asked him where the church was located and how long it would take to get the pews. He said the church is in Hickory, North

Carolina, and he gave me the address. A team of brothers and I took a U-Haul and retrieved the pews. The furniture was in excellent condition, but more than we could use or had space to place. One of the ministers said we had no place for all the pews, so we should get what we could use. I told him that we were taking them all.

We filled up the church building and stored the rest in my garage, while I had to park my cars in the driveway. I figured that was a minor inconvenience for the tremendous blessing we had received. About two years later, after God blessed us with another building, we were able to give the furniture to another church that needed it. I firmly believe that God always blesses us to be a blessing to others. Yes, just as I have felt, *"there were pews in the hills*!

> *The blessing of the LORD makes one rich, And He adds no sorrow with it.* (Prov 10:22)

> *Delight yourself also in the LORD, And He shall give you the desires of your heart.* (Ps 37:4)

When our delight in the Lord determines the desires in our heart, we can expect stuff to occur that we cannot fabricate.

GOD, THE COMPUTER-AIDED DESIGN SPECIALIST

Reflecting on my days at Bell Laboratories in New Jersey reminds me of the time I felt my lifetime dream had come true. I was working with pioneers in the computer industry. These men and women worked with those I studied about while in college. I worked under the technical staff who knew and worked with William Shockley, inventor of the transistor. His invention paved the way for the massive reduction in the size of computer components. Also, I got to meet men like James West, an African American inventor who holds several patents on the electret microphone.

People think it is strange when I say that the computer explosion did not begin with Steve Jobs of Apple or Bill Gates of Microsoft. The idea for their unique operating systems can be traced back to the inventors of the C programming language and the Unix operating system for mainframe computers that date back to the early 1960s at Bell Laboratories.

I owe my opportunity mainly to those who paved the way for programs such as affirmative action. Although I had prepared myself through hours of studying and time in the library, I would still not have been given the once-in-a-lifetime opportunity. If not for these programs, many people of color would have never received the opportunities that helped to level the *employment playing field*.

When I was hired in June 1978, the sophisticated microprocessor industry and development war were gaining steam. While still in college, I read an article in an electronic magazine about the plans for a 32-bit microprocessor that Bell Laboratories was designing. The report was exciting! I knew this was where I wanted to spend the rest of my life. From middle school through high school, I had to have the latest gadget. I would spend weeks selling flower seeds to purchase *one* transistor radio, wrist watches, and one transistor radio in the shape of a ballpoint pen. While reading the article, I knew that Bell Labs was the place for me, and no other career path even came close.

Little did I know that just months later, I would be working on a team designing a companion chip called a math accelerator Unit (MAU) to be a slave to the 32-bit microprocessor, still in the design phase. The magazine article made it sound like it was near completion. The MAU was designed to be a part of the finished circuitry for the 32-bit CPU. Without going into the boring details, the MAU was an integrated circuit to handle complex mathematical algorithms to relieve the central processor unit (CPU) of the math workload, significantly slowing down any computation.

My job, as a computer-aided design specialist, was to help design smaller circuits that would fit into the whole and be the. It was my dream job, and I loved what I did. I perfected my design for a stringless bass guitar. I built it, and it worked very well. I played it a few times in church while living in New Jersey.

Because of the competition brewing in the Silicon Valley and China, being first to announce a working 32-bit processor became the priority. We worked tirelessly, putting in long days and most of the night. It was nothing to show up at the labs the next day, walk down the long halls, pass a door, and spot an engineer sleeping under his desk, only to get up and continue to work. There were rumors outside of the lab that strange people were working inside the gated walls. Though one engineer walked backward due to an uncommon congenital disability in his knee, the rumor was that workers could be seen walking backward due to the unusual pressures of their jobs. It was easier for him to walk backward because his knee would be in pain and give out when he tried to walk the usual way.

My role on the project was to use a custom computer-aided design (CAD) program sophisticated enough to organize millions of transistors into what were called superblocks—each precisely arranged within a designated space and time frame. I came close to completing it, but there was one section where everything simply wouldn't fit. I spent days and countless hours trying to position the transistors in that area, but nothing worked. Even after getting advice from other CAD specialists, the problem remained unresolved. The computer program wouldn't simulate a working unit; no matter what I tried, the simulation would fail.

This day I tried until about 7 PM. Exhausted with an emerging migraine headache, I returned home to rest and start fresh the next day. As I drove down Highway 22 near Plainfield and Piscataway, New Jersey, I thought of the pressure I was under to complete my part of the project. Bell Labs had invested so heavily in a timely completion that *heads to roll* if something went wrong and we did not meet the deadline. As my anxiety increased and I drew closer to my home, I said under my breath, "Lord, please help me figure this out." It was not a particularly spiritual moment; it was something I learned to say growing up in a home where my mother was deeply pious and had a strong relationship with God. I don't know whether I believed the Lord would hear and help me. After all, why should He care if Bell Laboratories was first to develop a working chipset before anyone in Silicon Valley?

After a long, exhausting, and stressful day, I was glad to finally retire. It was about one o'clock in the morning, and I dreamed of the solution to the problem that had haunted me for days. I jumped out of bed and rushed to put on clothes. My wife said, "What are you doing, and where are you going?" Excited and afraid that I would forget it, I said as I hurried out of my pajamas into work clothes, "I dreamed the answer; I know what to do to make it work!" After arriving at the labs and sitting down at the green computer screen, I began to program what I saw in the dream. As the Fans on the digital electronic mainframes filled the room with hums and tunes of rotations, I put the transistors in the allotted spaces, ran the simulation, and it passed. This meant that it would be a working product when this chip went to the mask and into testing. After production, we had to fix one design error, but after that, the chip passed all the tests. The MAU marked a significant step toward enabling later CPUs to reach speeds required for advanced computational tasks.

I'm still not sure if God cares whether Bell

A Simple "Lord help me" saved my job.

Laboratories was successful. But I know that a simple "Lord help me" saved my job and laid the foundation for a promotion I received six months later. What I dreamed up is not something that I could make up. I continue to thank God for the raise I received to help support my growing family. To God be the Glory.

> *For the LORD God is a sun and shield: the LORD will give grace and glory: no good thing will he withhold from them that walk uprightly.* (Ps 84:11)

GOD, THE COMPUTER PROGRAMMING MASTER

I relocated to North Carolina and provided for my family, primarily through consulting in programming and installing computers. I was known as a Unix/Xenix operating specialist in the surrounding area, and by this time, had become proficient in some programming languages and would occasionally do some programming, though it was not my preferred thing to do.

I had recently taken on a client in Fort Mills, South Carolina, who was using a. Unix-based system with a custom accounting software package. Over the years, they had accumulated a large amount of stored data, but there was no efficient way to extract the specific information they needed. The program had been custom-built, but unfortunately, the original developers hadn't provided a way to manipulate the data for forecasting or analyzing past performance and sales.

As with any programmer, I did not need to know accounting to write an accounting program. All I needed was to talk to an accountant who could tell me what they were trying to achieve. The accountants in the office were not hopeful that they could get what they needed. But they were willing to pay $6000.00 if I could run the report.

I was the sole provider for my family, and consulting was my source of income. Though I was pastoring, the church's financial needs always came first. So, I vowed to support my family without depending on the church.

As I took on the task and I worked on it, I had the empirical evidence that no one knew computers and programming like the Lord. God taught me how to make money fixing computers and opened numerous doors to assure me that I had what I needed to provide for my family. So, I did what I had learned to do. I prayed and asked the Lord to guide me. I am always conscious of the Lord's will. It is in my heart to never hold God hostage to *only* helping me the way I desire. If he chooses not to give me the guidance and understanding to figure it out, then I have the words of 1 Thessalonians 5:18 to fall back on: *"In everything, give thanks: for this is the will of God in Christ Jesus concerning you."*

This time, the Lord granted me the favor of receiving the necessary funds. At about 5 o'clock one morning, I dreamed the answer to a particular algorithm and programming routine needed to search and find the data that fit their criteria. I wrote the routine and tested it in my at-home office. I went to the site early that morning and spent a few hours coding the program and helping run it, and retrieving the data.

I walked out of that place at about 2 PM with a Six-Thousand-dollar check made out to Ron, Inc. To God be the glory for the things that he does that no one can say, "you made that up!" Proverbs says it best:

The blessing of the LORD, it makes rich, and he adds no sorrow with it. (Prov 10:22)

I have told many young people who go off to college always to keep God, his church, and the fellowship of the saints a priority while away at college. For whatever we are studying, God is the expert. We put him first and let him be our tutor. I am not talking about something that I read or heard. I am speaking from personal experience. The many examples of my encounters could not be a coincidence or an accident. Divine providence is the only thing that makes any sense. After all these years, it would take more faith to believe that there is no God than it does to believe that there is a God. I can relate to the Psalmist, who concludes:

> *The fool has said in his heart, "There is no God." They are corrupt and have done abominable iniquity; There is none who does good.* (Ps 53:1)

It's one thing to verbalize an atheistic view because of what one is feeling at a particular time. However, it's another thing to say it from one's soul as a heartfelt conviction. To live in this orderly world for any amount of time and conclude that a beyond-intelligent designer is not behind it is stupid. This universe could have no more formed on its own than I could make up all the phenomena that have occurred in my life. But I am only one person sharing a few examples. Just think of the many God-fearing believers with even greater amazing testimonies of God's intervention. Again, I continue to say that my life is working for me because God is working in me to do His good pleasure.

I no longer focus on my imperfections and propensity to make bloopers and blunders because he remembers that we are dust (Ps 103:14). But He makes the end suitable for those who love him and are called according to his purpose. I encourage everyone to keep seeking the Lord while he may be found. He is in a class by Himself! When he stamps his signature on a thing, it will be something you cannot make up, but will keep you looking up and beyond the hills to receive providential help from the Lord's divine sanctuary.

TWO WIVES IN THE SAME CITY

In my nearly 40 years of pastoral ministry, this encounter ranks high on the list for paying a hefty price for not seeking divine guidance and checking with God before proceeding. The church was still worshiping in the building off BF Road. I would spend hours trying to repair or change something to be more presentable. So, it was not unusual for someone to drop in and want to talk or engage me in a theological conversation. This one individual was an adjunct professor at the nearby college.

He had stopped by several times before, and we had pleasant conversations about different themes. But this time, he appeared to be troubled in his spirit. With a sad countenance, he shared how his wife was sick and needed a procedure requiring finances that he did not have, so she could not have the procedure.

He sounded legitimate, since I knew he was an African who was here on assignment. The amount was significant, but I had a small available savings at the time. Also, integrity in ministry was an essential concern for me. I did not want to preach a message about God's love and helping those in need without practicing what I was preaching.

Since I felt as though I knew him, without a second thought, I went to the bank, withdrew the money, and gave it to him. Without reservation, I accept his promise to pay it back once his money comes through the following week.

I finished what I was doing and went home. I retired around 9:30 that night. During the night, I had a disturbing dream. I was preaching hard, and people were jumping and hollering throughout the little building. Suddenly, their jumping and shouting turned into an African dance. They formed a circle as they danced, but I was still preaching hard! Once they created the ring and made a few rotations, a giant demon rose out of the middle of the circle while I continued to preach.

The dream startled me, so I thought, "What have I done?" Somehow, I knew it was connected to the adjunct professor I lent the money to, as it was the day I went to his house as soon, but no one was there and it had been cleaned out. It was obvious that whoever lived there had vacated the premises in a hurry.

Now I'm concerned. Also, I knew his wife, who was a Caucasian woman. I spent the morning trying to figure out which hospital she was in as a patient. Nothing was working. So, I went to another place looking for where I thought he might be. By this time, it's almost 2 PM.

While trying to find him, I ran into her. I was shocked to see her out and about. I told her I was told that she had been hospitalized in need of an expensive procedure. She said nothing was wrong with her, and she did not know what he was talking about because she was not sick. But she went on to tell me about the problems she was experiencing. Both were leaders in a prominent church organization.

She confided that he was not who he appeared to be. Far from honest, he was a shrewd operator who had convinced their organization to fund vans for a ministry project he was allegedly doing. But it turned out to be nothing more than a scam.

What she told me next shed light on the dream that triggered my suspicion about him. She revealed that he was in line to become a chief in his home village in Africa. His family had sent him to France to receive an education at some of the best universities. Their goal was for him to return and take his position, but he was adamantly against doing it. However, a significant amount of funding was tied to the chief role within his community. The only way he could access these funds was to take his place among his people. While he was living in America, his parents continued to support him financially so he could further his education. But from time to time, he would travel back to Africa. She went on to say that whenever he returned to America, he seemed different. It was as if he had been involved in some form of witchcraft. She described strange markings on his back, resembling chicken scratches.

I could not find him, and she did not know where he was. He was supposed to be promoted within her church organization, but they were closing in on his questionable activities. Since her mother worked in the police department, his wife asked her to search for his name in their database. What she discovered shocked us. Though working at the college in Charlotte gave him a good cover, he was wanted in several East Coast states for running scams and extortion. But as more pieces of the puzzle came together, we uncovered that he was married to two women, both living in Charlotte. The other wife was seriously ill and preparing for a medical procedure, completely unaware of the double life he was living.

It would have been different if I had prayed before giving him the money. My dad taught me how to delay decisions by saying, "Let me think about it." But caught me off guard, I acted before allowing God to caution me. What I saw in the dream was a warning and rebuke. Wife number one confirmed that what the dream was showing me was that he was to become an African tribal chief. He would return to Africa and engage in the rituals to keep his finances flowing. I never saw him again, nor get the money back. In losing money, I gained a wealth of experience in acknowledging God in all my ways to receive the proper guidance. I was warned in my dream, but after I had given him the money.

> *I will bless the LORD, who hath given me counsel: my reins also instruct me in the night seasons.* (Psalm 16:7)

DIVINE PROVISION

Provision prə-ˈvi-zhən

The process of providing or state of being prepared
beforehand.

NO MONEY IS THE PROBLEM

> *... therefore, I will deliver all this great multitude into your*
> *hand, and you shall know that I am the LORD.* (1 Kgs
> 20:28)

At one time, I was desperately searching for another
place of worship for our growing congregation. The little
building we were in should have been condemned. After
I was there in obedience to my leader, we did what we
could to make it look presentable inside and out. But
because we are a foot-stomping, dancing group in our
expression of worship, we could not keep the dust from
constantly rising and settling on everything in the place.

So, I was constantly praying for God to give us a
better building. Traditionally, we wore white on the first
Sunday as we celebrated communion. No matter how
much we cleaned the building and washed down the pews,
we could not get them clean enough for dirt not to show
up on someone's white attire. I would always be
embarrassed when I noticed dirt on someone's white after
the service. So, I constantly prayed for God to help us in

that area. I dreamed about buildings and awoke to make sketches. Ironically, the Living Church Campus in Charlotte is like one of the sketches I dreamed.

The desire for a different place was so strong that I would transform every abandoned building I passed by into a church building in my mind. If I saw an abandoned car garage, I would envision how the front sliding doors could become a large wall with two large windows. If I passed an abandoned house, in my mind, I would imagine a steeple on the roof, extend the back to the sanctuary, and eventually allow the house part to be the offices.

I had an African American real estate agent looking for us. He found a potential place, and he took me to it. A Muslim group was selling its facility. The real estate agent picked me up in his beautiful black Cadillac and took me to the property. The building was probably a minor improvement over where we were, but it would require too much work to purchase and then get it ready to use. I told him it was not what we were looking for. They were asking a reasonable price for it, but I did not feel that this was something we should pursue further.

The real estate agent was disappointed because he was trying to unload this place. He knew that we were desperate for anything that we could find. Seeing this place, I realized we were not as hopeless as it seemed. Also, beggars "can be choosy" when they serve a merciful God. As the

"Beggars who serve a merciful God can be choosy."

agent smoked his pipe, his response was surprising. His exact words were, "The problem with some people is that they have no money. "Now, that would have been offensive, even embarrassing, except I served a God who does not need me to have all the money before he blesses me. His promises to supply the need are based on His riches in glory and not my riches in the bank account. But this was still fresh in my mind for another reason.

A few weeks earlier, I had preached a message entitled, "He's God no matter where you are," using 1 Kings chapter 20. The message was about a time in the life of King Ahab, and Israel's army fought off an attack launched by the Syrians. Although outnumbered, Israel defeated them because God gave Ahab and Israel's military the victory. Ahab was not popular at the time because of decisions that he had made, such as his marriage to Jezebel, a committed Baal worshiper. But the Syrian army was pitting their gods against the God of Israel. So the fight was no longer about who had the best army, but who served the real God. The Syrians attacked Jerusalem, which sits on a hill. When Israel's army defeated them, the Syrians attributed their defeat to the battle's location.

Then the servants of the king of Syria said to him, "Their gods are gods of the hills. Therefore, they were stronger than we; but if we fight against them in the plain, surely we will be stronger than they. (1 Kgs 20:23)

Then a man of God came and spoke to the king of Israel, and said, "Thus says the LORD: 'Because the Syrians have said, "The LORD is God of the hills, but He is not God of the valleys," therefore I will deliver all this great multitude into your hand, and you shall know that I am the LORD. (1 Kgs 20:28)

The agent was partially right. We did not have nearly enough money that a bank would require, and the price of commercial real estate in Charlotte and the surrounding areas was beginning to rise sharply. But when the agent spoke those words, I knew he challenged our God to work for us! I remember this like it happened yesterday. A smile came on my face when he said those words because I knew he had blessed me by challenging my God. He taught me that when no money is the problem, it's good to serve a God who takes "no money" as His opportunity and a down payment on His glory. God gets to throw His weight around and receive all the credit for doing it. To say it more spiritually, for the agent to suggest that this was the best we could do because we had no money was an opportunity for our God to receive the glory by showing us the best He was willing to do for us.

My desire was to have a presentable place to corporately worship Him. I knew we could serve God anywhere because true spiritual worship only depends on devotion, not location. However, I refused to live in a nice brick home, drive a decent car, and worship God in a place that was less than my residence and vehicle. I was never satisfied worshiping God in a place that was not as nice and comfortable as my home and car.

The building where we were worshipping needed a complete do-over. Since we were renting, we were limited in what we could do. A biblical principle that I take very seriously drove my determination: the worship offered to God should be the best I can offer Him. I believe the genesis of all things defines this. The Scriptural account of the worship of the first two sons highlights this idea:

> *And in the process of time, it came to pass that Cain brought an offering of the fruit of the ground to the LORD. Abel also brought of the firstborn of his flock and of their fat. And the LORD respected Abel and his offering.* (Gen 4:3-4)

Cain brought *an offering*, but Abel *brought the firstborn*. It did not make a difference whether it was fruit or flock, but Abel brought his firstborn, and Cain brought something. It did not say that Cain brought his first fruit, which would have been equivalent to Abel's firstborn. God deserves and expects our first and best because it confirms our faith in Him to bless us with the rest. "You cannot have a first unless there will be a second and beyond."

Because I felt this so strongly, I saved the tithes that people gave towards a down payment on the facility that

I hoped God would provide, The time finally came for us where "no money" was a problem, but it was not our problem because we serve a God who has never had a problem, only a plan and a purpose. Just as the Syrians spoke words that positioned Ahab and Israel up for God to come through, this real estate agent spoke words that set us up for God to come through on our behalf, though we do not have enough money. Still, God does not need our funds to be in our pocket; He only needs our love for Him to be in our heart.

> *And we know that all things work together for good to them that love God, to them who are the called according to **his** purpose* (Rom 8:28)

When our love for him supports God's purpose for us, things will occur that we cannot make up

WHEN GOD SAYS YES, NO IS FORBIDDEN

This was the only time I have ever dreamed in color. It was about owning another Conversion van. In the dream, I saw the color of the van. In the past, I had owned vans but downsized when I moved back south. However, one night, I dreamed that we had purchased another van for my family. In the dream, I saw a "Ford Econoline van. I even saw the van in color. I later told my wife that I wanted to get another van since the children were at the age where the extra room would be comfortable. The ministry kept us traveling to different places.

I picked up a free car trader magazine and flipped through it, looking for a van. I saw a picture of a van like the one in my dream. When I went to see it, it was the same color I had seen in my dream." It had an extended roof and was customized inside and outside. The actual van had more features on the outside, but the body style was the same as I saw it in the dream. The van had low mileage and looked practically new.

Since the seller was a bank vice president, the transaction was easy because he ensured I received the loan approval. After we closed the deal and filled out the paperwork, I shared my desire for a place to purchase as a sanctuary. I told him that we might need his help later and asked if I could contact Him. He said, Yes, Ron, give me a call."

Less than three years later, I was driving down Harris Boulevard and spotted this church property with a for sale sign out front. I looped back to get a closer look. I took down the information, called them, and set up an appointment to see the inside.

We needed $40,000 but only had 15,000.

When an older congregation member and I went to see it, we felt it was ideal. The purchase price was $200,00, and banks would only finance 80% or $160,000, but we only had fifteen thousand dollars. We came up with another five thousand, but still needed another twenty thousand dollars. Since someone else was looking at the property, ready to make a down payment, we were running out of time.

With less than four business days to offer a letter of intent to buy, we needed the bank to go another 10%. I remembered my conversation with the bank vice president. So I called him and reminded him of who I was and what I needed. He responded to me, "Yes, Ron, we will take a look at it, and we will help you." He gave me the name of the loan officer inside the bank to contact. I spoke to him and told him what we needed. I told him the bank's limit was 80%, but we needed at least 90%. He said that the bank could not do that. I said to Him, "But TI noted that the bank would help us. His exact words, with a sarcastic tone, were, "Mr. TI is not doing this, I am doing this, and I'm telling you that we do not do that for anybody."

My response may have offended him, or he had other reasons for his almost demeaning hostility. After I hung up. I tried to figure out different ways to get the rest of the money. This conversation was on a Thursday. We had until Tuesday of the following week to have a letter of intent to the owners. By that Saturday, I had practically given up hope of coming up with another $20,000. That Sunday, I went to church and preached like I usually do; it was a long day for us, so I was exhausted when I came home.

I loved watching the Jimmy Swaggart ministry broadcast on Sunday night. The way he played the piano would always minister to me and calm my spirit. This night, I desperately needed my soul to be settled. I was still bothered by being unable to come up with another $20,000 to purchase the property. The words of the real estate agent came into my mind, and I began to feel he was right: "The problem with some people is that they have no money." In retrospect, when we are down, our adversary will seize every opportunity to remind us why we should go further down.

I fell asleep watching television, listening to Jimmy Swagart sing and play the piano. This occurred when stations raised the volume during commercials and special announcements. I slept from about 8:15 to 11 PM. The time came for the Eyewitness News hour. When it came on with breaking news, the volume was raised. The loudness and introductory music startled me out of deep sleep. The announcer said, "Breaking News, a triathlon accident at TC South Carolina, and a man lost his life. "I woke up and sat in bed to watch the rest of the story. They went to the commercial break after the announcement.

When it came time for the story, they talked about what had occurred earlier that day at a triathlon event where someone had lost their life. They called the name, and his name sounded familiar. As they continued to talk, I realized that the man had the same name as the loan officer I spoke to on Thursday. I said out loud, "That's my loan officer!" It was shocking, and I was still not sure. What was the chance that the person I had spoken with on Thursday would be in the news just three days later? No, I was not sure if it was the same person.

So the next day, as soon as the bank opened, I called. I asked the receptionist if I could speak with the vice president I knew. He came to the phone to speak to me. I asked him if the person who lost his life was the loan officer from their bank. His exact"(country) words were, "Yeah, we are devastated around here. But I will take your loan application and get you the intent letter to give to the property owners tomorrow."

This unfortunate turn of events meant we could secure the finances for the property we did not have enough money to purchase it. Because of the death of the loan officer who adamantly told us no, the one who told me yes came back into the picture to complete the loan.

Saying you cannot make this stuff up is an understatement. Since then, God has blessed us to build a learning center on the property and secure other properties in other locations. Because God had already said yes, how it unfolded was left to Him. To God be the glory. I have this story because of God's glory. When God is getting His glory, we experience miracles no one could ever make up.

Commit your way to the LORD, Trust also in Him,
And He shall bring it to pass. (Ps 37:5)

If we entrust our way to God as an affirmation of our trust in Him, impossible things will happen that we cannot make up.

IF YOU HAVE A NEED, SOW A SEED

Now he who supplies seed to the sower and bread for food will also supply and increase your store of seed and will enlarge the harvest of your righteousness. (2 Cor 9:10)

My wife and I envisioned a learning center on the 3.5 remaining acres of the church property. Her vision was the school, but I also envisioned recreational facilities such as a basketball court as a place where people can gather and experience discipleship in action. Through an act of God, I could not make our vision become a reality.

When it came to the needs of the ministry, I always felt that if God were in on what was happening, eventually, He would sign off on it without harassing or holding the membership hostage to a financial obligation. Do I believe that it is more blessed to give than to receive? Yes, I do. But equally, I believe the proverb that says:

There is a way that appears to be right, but in the end, it leads to death. (Prov 16:25 NIV 2011)

God's way is always the right way, and not everything that appears right leads to more life. The last thing I want is to kill aspects of a ministry by obligating people in ways they may not be able to maintain. People come and go within a ministry, but the financial needs remain the same. So, my goal in financing a new building project was to do it so that it would not obligate people for a certain amount for an extended period. I believe that if God approves a move, the resources will become available as we walk by faith.

We had the plans and desire, but did not have a financial agreement with a bank that suited my objective. When banks see churches, they automatically want to know the number of giving entities and a host of other information. Securing a loan for the project was not a problem, but deciding how we wanted to secure the loan was. The bank was willing to work with us based on the approach of giving units pledging a certain amount. I refused to do it that way because I believed that God had another way.

By this time, God had blessed us with a financial reserve in the bank, which gave us some leverage at the negotiation table. However, I couldn't agree to any terms that required members to make personal financial commitments. I had already seen God move on people's hearts to meet previous financial needs, and I trusted Him to do it again.

While we were still in the midst of negotiations—waiting, wondering, and trying to figure out how to fund the project—a pastor from a sister congregation needed financial help to secure heating for their building before winter. The amount he requested was significant, and granting it would have raised concerns with the bank that was working with us. I told him I would love to help him, but we could not touch our reserves because we were trying to complete our assignment, and touching those funds would jeopardize what God was helping us build.

Later, as I talked to my wife, she asked me about the meeting with the pastor. I shared what he wanted, but we could not risk doing it without jeopardizing our loan. She offered to let the women's auxiliary do it." Because they did so much for the ministry, I allowed them to have their separate account to do things around the church. When she said that, it flipped the male switch in my mind, and I reasoned that whether from the women's money or the general account, it is coming from the same pot. So, the overall number is still going to shrink noticeably.

By this time, my wife and I had an unspoken agreement that when it came to supporting the ministry and helping others in ministry, nothing that was within our power to do was off the table. We had the money to lend, and it was within our ability to do so. I agreed to allow the women's auxiliary to help the sister church make the needed.

Less than a month later, something occurred that we had been trying for months to work out. A representative from the bank called and said they had come up with a way to make it happen our way. They would hold our reserve as backup collateral in place of written commitments from pledges and giving units. This was ideal because it protected our reserves. The bank funded the project and required no extra signatures or personal obligations from the board of trustees.

God was waiting for us to sow a seed into someone else's ministry so he could meet our need. I tremble at the thought that I almost missed my blessing because I had not been willing to take the chance on losing money. Instead, I tried to make sense of why that amount should be withdrawn from our account, even if it was marked for the Women's auxiliary. My wife did not see it as taking a chance on losing anything, but as an opportunity to bless someone in need.

When this blessing came, I thought of Peter, who got out of the boat to take a stab at walking on water to get to Jesus. Yes, he started sinking, but for however long, he experienced what it felt like to walk on water.

Sometimes we try to get to Jesus, but refuse to get out of the boat to see the impossible made possible. Through this experience, God taught me that to walk on water, we must be willing to get out of the boat.

But this I say: He who sows sparingly will also reap sparingly, and he who sows bountifully will also reap bountifully. (2 Cor 9:6)

I'M SUPPOSED TO GIVE YOU THIS

One Sunday morning, the church had an unexpected financial need. As I was getting dressed for service, it was so heavily on my mind that I kneeled by the bathtub and said, "Lord, Please." I had no recourse or time to raise the needed funds. Usually, when I must preach, I have a one-track mind. Once I prayed, I had to focus on the message for that morning. When I arrived at church, I went to my office and prepared to go out to the sanctuary. Someone brought me an announcement and walked about 20 feet, turned around, and returned to me. She handed me an envelope, but since I was on my way to the pulpit, I only had time to stick the envelope in my pocket.

That night, when I got home and was undressing, I felt the envelope in my coat pocket. When I took it out and opened it, there was a check for a little more than what we needed to pay the bill. To God Be the Glory! This is miraculous stuff you can't make up!

PANDEMIC NOT PANDEMONIUM

During the Pandemic, we were out of our building for nearly two years. Like so many congregations, both of our locations took a membership dive. In my pastoral tenure, I have witnessed the " walking by faith and not by sight." However, those who keep walking by faith will eventually walk into a place where the sight is clear, as has been my case as senior pastor.

As I write this, the congregation is slowly recovering. But when it comes to provision, we saw an increase and support from unexpected sources. More importantly, God had given First Lady Parson a vision of an early morning prayer conference call approximately ten years before the Pandemic. For ten years, five mornings each week, a team of prayer warriors awoke at 5 a.m. to bombard heaven for an hour with petitions, praise, and thanksgiving. They targeted specific prayer requests and groups that they identified and carried to the throne of grace. When the Pandemic hit, our prayer time was already a function of a prayer mind.

We had begun online giving about four years before the Pandemic. Since we were already established in our online giving, we could bring others up to speed in being proficient in online giving. The Lord still blesses us to be a blessing and goes before us to prepare our way. Divine providence and provision protected our ministry from spiritually or financially going under during the Pandemic.

In early 2022, God provided in ways only He could at our newly purchased location. Before the Pandemic, we had agreed with the previous owner to rent the property with the option to buy in three years. The third year coincided with the first year of the Pandemic. Although the membership was down, we prayerfully took a leap of faith and purchased the real estate, including the church building.

Shortly after the purchase, an anonymous donor left a five-thousand-dollar cash donation. Initially, I thought, Do not ask any questions, just put it in the offering. It may be a drug deal gone wrong, and God had blessed us when we needed it the most. I generally seek biblical precedent for my actions concerning finances. I thought about **Proverbs 13:22, "…** and the wealth of the sinner *is* laid up for the just." If, by chance, this was the case, I chose to apply the principle of **1 Corinthians 10:25-26** "Eat whatever is sold in the meat market, asking no questions for conscience' sake;" for *"the earth is the LORD'S, and all its fullness."*

About three weeks later, probably the same person, left another envelope containing twenty-five hundred dollars. We walked by faith to purchase this property during the Pandemic. As my niece often says, "Look at God." Shortly after, we had another miraculous intervention. With the purchase of an older building, there are always unforeseen repairs and things that need replacing. One of the heating units servicing the fellowship Hall required repair. When we got a three-thousand-dollar quote from our HVAC specialist, even he felt sticker shock.

We received the estimate on a Saturday, so we called our newly installed Pastor and told him the price. After he heard the cost, he laughed. This did not seem appropriate, but he texted us the reason for his positive response. Seemingly out of nowhere, he had received a Cash App transaction earlier that day. Someone decided to bless and tithe three thousand dollars to that Living Church *(Cash APP)* account —the exact cost of the repairs. The new pastor put at the bottom of the text, "You cannot make this stuff up."

For me, "out of nowhere" and "out of no way" are expressions that reflect divine providence—signs that God's provision and protection remain constant for those who love Him. The Pandemic has not been pandemonium for us. Although we were out of the physical building, the church kkkkkkkk,,,,olmaintained its obligations without interruptions as God supplied our needs according to His riches in glory!

CONCLUSION

An aged David looked back over his eventful life, and he concluded,

Surely goodness and mercy shall follow me all the days of my life: and I will dwell in the house of the LORD forever. (Ps 23:6)

When I look in the rear-view mirror of my life and ministry, I see goodness and mercy following me. Our Lord orders the steps of a good man (Ps. 37:23). Jesus challenged the notion of being called good (Mk. 10:18) unless He is God in the flesh. Scripture states there is none good apart from God (Ps. 14:3, 53:3). In Jesus, that goodness continues in the word that became flesh (Jn. 1). Our goodness is a function of Christ living within us. Our goodness is as good as it can get when we allow the spirit of Christ to live within us to guide us in the good ways of God. In God, it's all good even when we are having a bad day!

According to the Psalmist, the Lord "leads [us] in the paths of righteousness for His name's sake," even when that path is "through the valley and the shadow of death" (Ps. 23). Often, God's map shows only the mountain peaks of where we are going. But between those mountains are valleys with unknown challenges, pitfalls, and puzzling occurrences that require the Lord's rod and his staff to comfort us. These are **protection** from danger as He keeps us on a safe path. That protection will include God disciplining, directing, and keeping us on the right track, in sometimes painful ways. As we continue the journey, in His **provision,** he prepares a table before us in the presence of our enemies (Ps. 23:5). For His providence is purposeful and intentional. God knows exactly where we are going. We are puzzled as God puts the pieces of our lives into place. Divine guidance doesn't always inform us of where we're going. As humans who have to die daily, we sometimes take the wrong turn, thinking that we heard God. Then we find ourselves on a dead-end street, especially when we hear the word and see the signs, but choose to ignore them.

God declares the end from the beginning (Isa. 46:10). Therefore, all the pieces of the puzzle box of our life fit perfectly together, and God takes His time to put each piece where it belongs. Only he knows the infinitely large *scheme of his things* and is slowly, but surely, working out what we are desperately trying to figure out.

Nothing catches Him by surprise! Yet, we must intentionally work out our salvation while trusting God to work in us to do His good pleasure (Phil 2:13). Whatever pleases Him will be good *for us*, even when it looks abysmal.

Our role is to love Him, as He loves *us*! Like puzzle construction, every piece of our life will eventually fit in its proper place and serve its purpose.

Everything is appropriate in its own time. But though God has planted eternity in the hearts of men, even so, many cannot see the whole scope of God's work from beginning to end." Eccl 3:11 (TLB)

Since the *pieces* of our life are in the hands of God, given time, that which is puzzling to us inside the box of life will resemble the picture on the front of the box. He is putting each piece together, and only he sees how the image on the outside comes to be of the box before it is complete. In the meantime, we must trust Him and His timing because it's impossible to see and think outside the box that contains us.

Whenever we are afraid, disarrayed, or knocked down by life, God knows where the pieces fit. While we are quick to tell others to "pick up the pieces and go on," we are often unable to figure out how things like the untimely death of a young mother with small children fit into the place of our lives. In those times when we cannot find the pieces, God always knows where they are and where they fit. In God's own time, He heals all wounds and reveals what is true.

For now, we see in a mirror, dimly, but then face to face. (1 Cor 13:12)

Love and trust God, and things will occur that we cannot make up, but will keep us looking up for providence, protection, and provision.

Now to Him who is able to do exceedingly abundantly above all that we ask or think, according to the power that works in us, to Him be glory in the church by Christ Jesus to all generations, forever and ever. Amen. (Eph 3:20-21)

Ω

Notes

Notes

Notes

About the Author

Apostle Ronnie L Parson serves a Presiding Apostle of the Church of the lord Jesus Christ of the Apostolic Faith and the Senior Pastor of The Living Church Ministries in Charlotte and Statesville, North Carolina. Has held several key denominational leadership positions over many years including serving as head of its Counseling Department, Diocesan Bishop, Executive Secretary and Apostle of Global Missions.

He holds an Associate. Degree in Electrical Engineering Technology, a Bachelor of Biblical Studies from Lee University. a Master of Theology & Arts in Christian Counseling and a Doctorate in Marriage and Family Counseling and from Gordon-Conwell Theological Seminary, He has taught pastoral counseling and theology at William L Bonner College.

Parson has authored several books and pamphlets on topics including marriage counseling, ministry leadership, and navigating faith in contemporary society. He and his wife, Rubina, regularly teach at leadership and marriage seminars and conduct conferences on contemporary theological themes impacting the 21st-century church.

As we all grow old, and facts become obscured, and even fables are told. Let these real accounts of God's divine providence, protection, and provision be a record for future generations that Jesus Christ is the same yesterday, today, and forever.

Ronnie Parson

www.ingramcontent.com/pod-product-compliance
Lightning Source LLC
Chambersburg PA
CBHW071017120626
46546CB00003B/1121